D0857125

THE RISE OF URBAN AMERICA

ADVISORY EDITOR
Richard C. Wade
PROFESSOR OF AMERICAN HISTORY
UNIVERSITY OF CHICAGO

GV 53
.S7
1970

AMERICANS
AT PLAY

Jesse Frederick Steiner

ARNO PRESS
&
The New York Times

NEW YORK · 1970

JUL 5 1972

INDIANA
PURDUE
LIBRARY
JUN   1972

FORT WAYNE

Reprint Edition 1970 by Arno Press Inc.

Reprinted from a copy in The University of Illinois Library

LC# 73-112574
ISBN 0-405-02476-2

THE RISE OF URBAN AMERICA
ISBN for complete set 0-405-02430-4

Manufactured in the United States of America

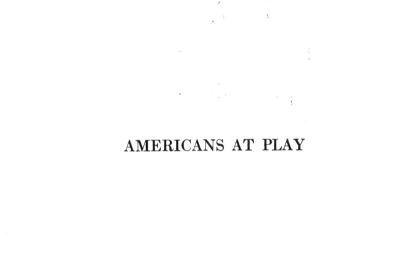

AMERICANS AT PLAY

MONOGRAPHS

RECENT SOCIAL TRENDS IN THE UNITED STATES

A Series of Monographs Prepared under the Direction of the President's Research Committee on Social Trends

Thompson and Whelpton—
POPULATION TRENDS IN THE UNITED STATES

Willey and Rice—
COMMUNICATION AGENCIES AND SOCIAL LIFE

Judd—
PROBLEMS OF EDUCATION IN THE UNITED STATES

McKenzie—
THE METROPOLITAN COMMUNITY

Brunner and Kolb—
RURAL SOCIAL TRENDS

Woofter—
RACES AND ETHNIC GROUPS IN AMERICAN LIFE

Breckinridge—
POLITICAL, SOCIAL AND ECONOMIC ACTIVITIES OF WOMEN

Wolman and Peck—
LABOR IN THE NATIONAL LIFE

Steiner—
AMERICANS AT PLAY

Keppel and Duffus—
THE ARTS IN AMERICAN LIFE

Sydenstricker—
HEALTH AND ENVIRONMENT

White—
TRENDS IN PUBLIC ADMINISTRATION

Wooddy—
GROWTH OF THE FEDERAL GOVERNMENT—1915–1932

AMERICANS AT PLAY

*Recent Trends in Recreation and
Leisure Time Activities*

BY

JESSE FREDERICK STEINER
Professor of Sociology, University of Washington

McGRAW-HILL BOOK COMPANY, INC.
NEW YORK AND LONDON
1933

President's Research Committee on
Social Trends
WESLEY C. MITCHELL, *Chairman*
CHARLES E. MERRIAM, *Vice-Chairman*
SHELBY M. HARRISON, *Secretary-Treasurer*
ALICE HAMILTON
HOWARD W. ODUM
WILLIAM F. OGBURN

Executive Staff
WILLIAM F. OGBURN, *Director of Research*
HOWARD W. ODUM, *Assistant Director of Research*
EDWARD EYRE HUNT, *Executive Secretary*

COPYRIGHT, 1933, BY THE
PRESIDENT'S RESEARCH COMMITTEE ON SOCIAL TRENDS

PRINTED IN THE UNITED STATES OF AMERICA

THE MAPLE PRESS COMPANY, YORK, PA.

FOREWORD BY THE COMMITTEE

AMERICANS AT PLAY by Jesse F. Steiner is one of a series of monographs published under the direction of the President's Research Committee on Social Trends, embodying scientific information assembled for the use of the Committee in the preparation of its report entitled *Recent Social Trends in the United States.*

The Committee was named by President Herbert Hoover in December, 1929, to survey social changes in this country in order to throw light on the emerging problems which now confront or which may be expected later to confront the people of the United States. The undertaking is unique in our history. For the first time the head of the Nation has called upon a group of social scientists to sponsor and direct a broad scientific study of the factors of change in modern society.

Funds for the researches were granted by the Rockefeller Foundation, an expert staff was recruited from universities and other scientific institutions, and a series of investigations was begun early in 1930 and concluded in 1932. The complete report contains the findings of the President's Research Committee on Social Trends together with twenty-nine chapters prepared by experts in the various fields.

Modern social life is so closely integrated as a whole that no change can occur in any of its phases without affecting other phases in some measure. Social problems arise largely from such unplanned reactions of the rapidly changing phases of social life upon the more stable phases. To give a few examples: changes in industrial technique react upon employment, changes in the character of adult work affect educational needs, changes in international relations affect domestic politics, changes in immigration policy affect the growth of population and the demand for farm products, changes in consumption habits affect the demand for leisure and facilities for enjoying it, changes in demands for social service by governmental agencies affect taxes and public debts, changes in methods of communication tend to standardize the mode of life in country and city. The effects noted in this list of illustrations in their turn cause other changes, and so on without assignable limits.

The usual practice of concentrating attention upon one social problem at a time often betrays us into overlooking these intricate relations. Even when we find what appears to be a satisfactory solution of a single problem, we are likely to produce new problems by putting that solution into practice. Hence the need of making a comprehensive survey of the many social changes which are proceeding simultaneously, with an eye to their reactions upon one another. That task is attempted in the Committee's report. Of course the list of changes there considered is not exhaustive. Nor can all the subtle interactions among social changes be traced.

To safeguard the conclusions against bias, the researches were restricted to the analysis of objective data. Since the available data do not cover all phases of the many subjects studied, it was often impossible to answer questions of keen interest. But what is set forth has been made as trustworthy as the staff could make it by careful checking with factual records. Discussions which are not limited by the severe requirements of scientific method have their uses, which the Committee rates highly. Yet an investigation initiated by the President in the hope that the findings may be of service in dealing with the national problems of today and tomorrow, should be kept as free as possible from emotional coloring and unverifiable conjectures. Accuracy and reliability are more important in such an undertaking than liveliness or zeal to do good. If men and women of all shades of opinion from extreme conservatism to extreme radicalism can find a common basis of secure knowledge to build upon, the social changes of the future may be brought in larger measure under the control of social intelligence.

FOREWORD

The Committee's researches were not confined to preparing a general report laid out with proper regard for balance. Intensive investigations of considerable length were carried out in several directions where the importance of the subjects warranted and adequate data were available. Some investigators were rewarded by especially valuable developments of their programs on a scale which made it impossible to condense the results into a single chapter without serious loss. In these cases separate monographs are necessary to provide adequate presentation of the evidence and the findings. However, at least a part of the subject matter of each monograph is dealt with in the Committee's general report, which should be read by all who wish to see a rounded picture of social trends.

PREFACE

During recent years people have become much concerned with the recreational side of life and insist far more than in the past upon easy access to sports, amusements, and other leisure time diversions of a widely varied nature. While recreation has always been a matter of deep human interest, it now occupies a more fully accepted position in the scheme of human affairs and finds ready justification on the grounds of health and efficiency as well as relief from the routine of daily toil. In a very real sense recreation has forged to the front as one of the compelling interests in human life and has already developed to the point where it makes extraordinary demands upon time and energy and requires large financial expenditures to cover its mounting costs.

Within this rapidly expanding field of recreational activities important changes are constantly taking place which are intimately bound up with the whole social and economic structure. The purpose of this volume is to study some of these more significant developments in order to determine if possible the direction the movement is taking. In this study of recent recreational trends it has not been possible to cover the entire field of leisure, which reaches out in many directions and includes an exceedingly wide range of activities. For purposes of this investigation emphasis has been placed primarily upon parks and playgrounds, competitive sports and games, commercial amusements, leisure time clubs and associations, pleasure travel, and the varied activities associated with outdoor vacation life. Consideration has not been given to the intellectual and cultural leisure time pursuits such as reading, art, music, drama, and other interests of a similar nature. Very little attention also has been given to what might be called private ways of spending leisure as for example informal calling and entertaining, amateur photography, stamp collecting, and the innumerable other hobbies and simple diversions that play such a large role in the daily lives of many people. Even within the specific phases of recreation chosen for study it has been necessary to limit attention to the more significant types of activities which may be regarded as fairly typical of the whole situation. Nevertheless, in spite of these limitations as to scope, this study, it is believed, is sufficiently comprehensive to give a fairly adequate picture of the more important recreational trends during recent years.

In contrast with much of the literature in this field, this volume is not concerned with the promotion of any recreational program nor does it attempt to appraise the value of the different types of recreational activities. Its distinctive feature is its effort to assemble from all available sources the materials that would throw light on the recent progress in recreation and give some indication of its present trends. In so far as possible it presents the quantitative data not only needed for determining the present status but useful also as a benchmark or basis for the measurement of future growth. The unfortunate gaps and inadequacies in the statistical materials are due at least partially to the lack of satisfactory records of recreational pursuits over a period of years. Existing recreational records are for the most part concerned with victories and championships rather than with growth of facilities, number of participants, and per capita costs. With no central authority responsible for the compilation of comprehensive data in the field of recreation, it has been a difficult and time consuming task to bring together the materials used in this study.

In the preparation of this volume valuable assistance has been received from many persons and organizations. Special mention should be made of the staff of the National Recreation Association who gave free access to their files and unpublished materials. The author is deeply indebted to

Professor E. W. Montgomery of the University of Kentucky who assisted in the collection and tabulation of the statistical data and contributed the chapter on rural recreation. Special thanks are also due Professor Malcolm M. Willey of the University of Minnesota who read the entire manuscript and offered many helpful criticisms and suggestions.

JESSE F. STEINER

UNIVERSITY OF WASHINGTON,
February, 1933.

CONTENTS

[xiii]

CONTENTS

AMERICANS AT PLAY

CHAPTER I

BACKGROUNDS AND BEGINNINGS OF AMERICAN RECREATION

THE present widespread interest in ways and means of enjoying leisure stands in striking contrast to earlier attitudes toward leisure and its uses. The rigors of our pioneer days gave little room for the development of leisure time activities. The hard struggle to conquer the wilderness and provide the necessities of life was too severe to give much attention to play. The uncertain outcome of this struggle and the constant dangers faced added zest to this life of toil and furnished in some measure the emotional outlet now sought in amusements and competitive sports.

Under such conditions it was natural to develop a philosophy of life that would exalt labor and look askance at unproductive activities. The idea that play was a form of idleness took such deep root in colonial times that even the play of children was frowned upon as undesirable. The Puritan revolt against the pleasures of life gave religious support to this philosophy of work and was a powerful factor in retarding the growth of recreational programs. The so-called worldly amusements were to be shunned in the interests of a higher goal in life. While this identification of pleasure with worldliness never won complete support, the influence of this point of view was far flung and even at the present time has not entirely disappeared.

Colonial Amusements.—Dominated by their ideas of the righteousness of labor and the sinfulness of useless diversions, the pioneers of America built up a world in

[1]

which leisure and sport were forced as far as possible into the background. Nevertheless, escape from the strong lure of interesting diversions was a difficult matter and it is easy for the present generation to exaggerate the lack of pleasurable recreation of earlier days. At a time when Americans were an out-of-doors people struggling for a livelihood amid all the vicissitudes of nature, they were able to secure many of the thrills of sport while engaged in necessary industry. The pursuit of wild game held no less fascination for the hunter because his evening meal depended upon the results of the chase. Fishing furnished its moments of excitement even when followed as a means of livelihood. The rigors and hardships of pioneer conditions could not efface entirely the attractions of camp life and the lure of open spaces.

Moreover, the less thrilling activities of daily toil frequently furnished occasions for neighborhood play. Corn huskings, barn raisings, and quiltings are examples of cooperative labor which gave opportunity for social intercourse and were enlivened by tests of skill and strength. Gatherings of this sort in which play was a by-product of work were a highly valued form of recreation well adapted to the rural situation that gave them birth. Religious meetings, also, although dominated by a rigid theology and a serious outlook on life, became social occasions of real importance. In spite of the hard conditions of life that had to be faced, there was no dearth of the more simple pleasures which brought enjoyment during hours of work as well as of leisure.

In addition to these forms of recreation that grew out of pioneer conditions, some of the sporting customs of European peoples found their way to the American colonies and gained a considerable following among those not deterred by religious taboos. Bear and bull baiting and cock fighting were blood sports brought from abroad which became forms of diversion for the populace at colonial fairs and at other places where crowds gathered together. Cock fighting was especially popular in the southern colonies and persisted as a sport until finally banned by law. The fox hunt, a traditional sport among the English gentry, was transplanted to colonial America and was long popular among the plantation owners in the South. Horse racing as early as the seventeenth century was securely established in the American colonies and became more widespread as leisure and wealth increased. Along with hunting and fishing it stands out as one of the chief sports of the American people during the eighteenth and early part of the nineteenth century. The following notice published by the Virginia *Gazette* in 1739 gives contemporary evidence of the kind and variety of sports and amusements that provided entertainment at the southern colonial fairs of that period.

And for the Entertainment and Diversion of all Gentlemen and others that shall resort thereto, the following PRIZES are given to be contended for, at the Fair, viz. A good Hat to be cudgell'd for; and to be given to the Person that fairly wins it, by the common Rules of Play. A Saddle of 40 s. Value, to be run for, once round the Mile Course, adjacent to this city, by any Horse, Mare, or Gelding, carrying Horseman's Weight, and allowing Weight for Inches. A handsome Bridle to be given to the Horse that comes in Second. And a good Whip to the Horse that comes in Third. A Pair of Silver Buckles, Value 20 s. to be run for by Men, from the College to the Capitol. A Pair of Shoes to be given to him that comes in Second. And a Pair of Gloves to the Third. A Pair of Pumps to be danc'd for by Men. A handsome Firelock to be exercis'd for; and given to the Person that performs the Manual Exercise best. A Pig, with his Tail soap'd, to be run after; and to be given to the Person that catches him, and lifts him off the Ground fairly by the Tail. There will be several other Prizes given. And as the Fair is to hold three Days, there will be Horse racing, and a Variety of Diversions every Day; and the Prizes not here publicly mentioned (for want of Room) will be then publicly declared, and appropriated in the best Manner. The Horses that run for the Saddle, are to be enter'd before Ten o'Clock on Wednesday Morning next, with Mr. Henry Bowcock, in Williamsburg; those that are not Contributors, to pay 2s.6d at Entrance. The Horse that wins the Saddle, not to run for any other Prize this Fair. Proper Persons will be appointed to have the Direction and Management of the Fair, and to decide any Controversies that may happen, in relation to the Bounties and Prizes to be bestowed.[1]

[1] John Allen Krout, *Annals of American Sport*, p. 24, Pageant of America, Vol. 15, New Haven, Yale University Press, 1929. In the preparation of this

The vogue of sports and amusements varied in the different colonies; the Pennsylvania Quakers and the New England Puritans were the most straitlaced while the South enjoyed more freedom to indulge in popular diversions. Religious opposition retarded the growth of recreational activities both North and South but nowhere were they ruled out entirely. Men of wealth and leisure kept their blooded horses and were enthusiastic patrons of the races as well as followers of the chase. Among the common people individual contests of strength and skill provided amusement for both spectators and participants. Organized team games were almost entirely unknown and participation in athletic sports with the exception of wrestling, fighting and similar contests was limited to a very small number of people. The public spectacle, on the other hand, especially the horse race and the cock fight, attracted large numbers of people during this early period. All these diversions, however, ran counter to much of the public opinion of that day and had to make a place for themselves in spite of widespread opposition. Even in the few colleges that had been established there was no encouragement given to the development of games and sports. President Wheelock of Dartmouth recommended in 1771 that the "students turn the course of their diversions and exercises for their health to the practice of some manual arts, or cultivation of gardens and other lands, at the proper hours of leisure and intermissions from study." In an essay on the "Amusements and Punishments Proper for Schools" published in 1790, it was suggested that the "amusements of our youth shall consist of such exercises as will be most subservient to their future employments in life." Agricultural and mechanical employments were proposed as suitable means of diversion. The author quoted with approval the plan of the Methodist College in Maryland where "a large lot is divided between the scholars, and premiums adjudged to those who produce the most vege-

chapter the author has drawn heavily from the above volume and from F. G. Menke's *All Sports Record Book* (1932 edition).

tables from their grounds, or who keep them in the best order." "The Methodists," he adds, "have wisely banished every species of play from their college."[2]

Sports during the Nineteenth Century.—During the early half of the nineteenth century, America still retained many of the characteristics of a pioneer nation with vast areas unsettled, transportation inadequate, and rural ideas dominating the life of the people. Neither wealth nor leisure existed in sufficient measure to make possible much emphasis upon leisure time activities. Popular amusements followed in the main the patterns set during the colonial period and were looked upon with disfavor by many influential leaders. Despite all obstacles, however, some headway was made in the development of recreational facilities and in the organization of clubs interested in the promotion of sports. During the first two decades of the century summer resorts were constructed along the Jersey shore and became popular among the wealthy residents of the eastern cities. Saratoga Springs, New York, and White Sulphur Springs, Virginia, were fashionable watering places before 1825. As early as 1830 the Cincinnati Angling Club was organized and similar fishing clubs were formed in other cities about the middle of the century. In 1831 the Sportsmen's Club of Cincinnati carried on competitive shooting at wild pigeons and quails released from ground traps. The New York Yacht Club was organized in 1844 and conducted annual regattas that attracted wide attention. In 1851 this club sent a yacht to England to participate in the English races. Boat clubs and rowing associations became common during the forties and fifties and both amateur and professional rowing and sculling races were held. The first intercollegiate boat race between Harvard and Yale was held in 1852. The Knickerbocker Baseball Club was established in New York in 1845 and by 1858 there was a sufficient number of baseball players to form a National Association of Baseball Players. Ice

[2] U. S. Bureau of Education, Bulletin No. 5, *Physical Training in American Colleges*, 1885, pp. 15–17.

skating became popular in northern cities in the fifties. Skating clubs were formed and races and figure skating became prominent winter diversions. Professional foot-races were also a common diversion throughout the first half of the century. A newspaper account of such a race held at Hoboken in 1844 stated that "from the head of the quarter stretch quite around to the drawgate, the enclosed space was so densely crammed as to render it nearly impossible to clear a space wide enough for the pedestrians to run through. Thousands filled the stands, but it would have required the amphitheatre of Titus to have accommodated the crowd."[3]

These examples are sufficient to indicate the rising tide of sports and amusements which gained greater headway as the century advanced. For the most part they were mere beginnings by small groups of people and were by no means widely or securely established. Recreational activities were tolerated rather than encouraged during the first half of the nineteenth century. It was not until the decades immediately following the Civil War that popular interest in sports began to develop in a more widespread manner. Baseball had been a popular game among the Union troops and after their demobilization amateur teams were formed in many cities. In 1869 the leading ball club of Cincinnati became the first professional nine and two years later eight professional teams organized the National Association of Professional Baseball Players. The public took great interest in the rivalries of the professional teams and attended their games in growing numbers. Approximately 10,000 people witnessed the opening game in New York in 1886. In 1875 roller skating was introduced into America and soon gained wide popularity. It is estimated that $20,000,-000 were invested in roller skating properties by the year 1885. The skating rinks were patronized by both men and women and became social centers of importance in many places. The League of American Wheelmen was formed in 1880 and had a membership of more than 10,000 in 1886.

[3] Krout, *op. cit.*, p. 186.

Between 1883 and 1887 a great deal of publicity was given to a bicycle tour around the world carried out successfully by an American. During the nineties cycle clubs were organized in almost every city, long tours were undertaken, races held, and many thousands adopted bicycle riding as their daily recreation. In 1869 there were at least 15 yacht clubs holding annual regattas. Twenty years later there were more than 125 cruising and racing associations maintaining yachts of different kinds in the harbors along the Atlantic and Pacific coasts and the Great Lakes. Croquet was brought to America in the sixties and during the following two decades enjoyed wide vogue throughout the country. Its rise is of special significance since it was one of the first outdoor games freely participated in by both men and women. The first national croquet tournament was held in 1882. International cricket matches were played with Canadian teams in 1853 and with English teams in 1859. A national archery tournament was held in 1879 under the auspices of the National Archery Association. That same year shooting ranges were maintained by 144 rifle clubs affiliated with the National Rifle Association. The New York Athletic Club was established in 1868 to promote interest in track and field events. Similar clubs were organized in other large cities and prospered sufficiently to construct club buildings well equipped for sport and social activities of their members. The first intercollegiate track and field contests were held in 1874 and the following year the Intercollegiate Association of Amateur Athletes of America was organized. In 1887 the National Cross Country Association was formed to promote cross country races, which had been introduced from England a few years earlier. Walking contests were especially popular in the seventies. The sports journals of that time were filled with the exploits of both amateur and professional pedestrians, some of whom competed in races between distant cities. The first of the modern Olympic games, held in Athens in 1896, was attended by a team of American contestants who won a majority of the events. Outing and hiking clubs enjoyed a wide vogue during the eighties and nineties. Coney Island was a famous resort as early as the seventies with its dancing pavilions, shooting galleries, and side shows. The annual trek southward to winter resorts began to assume considerable proportions during the nineties. Growing interest in camping and outdoor life was also apparent at this time but was hampered by lack of transportation facilities. Football and baseball had become great public spectacles before the end of the century. Golf and tennis, destined later to sweep rapidly over the whole country, had gained a foothold before 1900.

Even this cursory review of the growth of sports and games makes it clear that the foundations of the modern recreational movement were broadly and effectively laid during the nineteenth century, and more especially during its closing decades. This century was a period of beginnings characterized by the gradual breakdown of traditional prejudices against play and amusements. It was a time of awakening of interest in the possibilities of leisure and of the building up of new patterns in recreational life. This movement went forward slowly, and as late as 1858 Oliver Wendell Holmes wrote this scathing criticism of the city youth of his day: "I am satisfied that such a set of black-coated, stiff-jointed, soft-muscled, paste-complexioned youth as we can boast in our Atlantic cities never before sprang from loins of Anglo-Saxon lineage . . . We have a few good boatmen, no good horsemen that I hear of, nothing remarkable, I believe, in cricketing, and as for any great athletic feat performed by a gentleman in these latitudes, society would drop a man who should run around the Common in five minutes."[4] While later in the century this urban indifference to athletic sports was much less apparent, the chief interest of the populace was in public spectacles rather than in active participation in the games themselves. It was professional and not amateur athletics that claimed a large share of public attention. The furore over college

[4] Quoted by Krout, *op. cit.*, p. 148.

athletics during the late eighties and nineties was brought about by inter-collegiate contests participated in by a comparatively small number of picked and highly trained athletes. There was no strong demand at that time for the development of intramural sports in which all the students could join. The stage was all set for the expansion of recreational activities among the mass of the people but the great advance in this direction did not take place until the opening decades of the twentieth century.

The Rise of Modern Recreation.—The spectacular development of modern recreation has gone along with the rising tide of industry and the growth of cities during the past forty years. The expansion of recreation has been a large city movement and has gained acceleration as urbanization has advanced. As long as Americans were occupied chiefly with land settlement and the exploitation of natural resources, there was neither opportunity nor great necessity for an elaborate system of leisure time activities. But with the growth of industry cities began to expand and the whole tempo of American life changed. In 1890 only 40 per cent of the American people lived in urban territory while in 1930 the urban residents constituted 56.2 per cent of the total population. Between 1890 and 1930 the number of cities over 100,000 grew from 28 to 93 while the population in cities of this class increased nearly 275 per cent. During this period increasing numbers of people hitherto accustomed to out-of-door life were forced to work in factories and live in crowded urban districts. As machinery improved, routine tasks became the common lot of workmen, thus adding greatly to the monotony of labor. With their work speeded up by the machine and their hours of labor measured by the time clock, there was little opportunity to mingle pleasure with toil as had been possible under more simple conditions of employment. The traditional amusements of a rural people became pitifully inadequate and unsatisfying for factory workers and for the large numbers of people caught in the meshes of the business and the industrial world.

[9]

One of the reactions to this advancing urbanization has been the demand for shorter hours of labor so that more leisure would be available at the close of the working day. During the past fifty years the normal work-week in American industry has been reduced approximately 20 hours.[5] The amount of leisure that has been attained varies with different industries and with different grades of employment, but for nearly all classes the long hours of an earlier generation has been decreased to a marked degree. Moreover, annual vacations of a week to a month in length have become more widespread and modern inventions have lightened the toil of those engaged in the daily tasks of the home. The advance of machine industry has been marked by an expansion of leisure which would have been regarded as impossible at the beginning of the industrial revolution. It has been within this new world of leisure that modern recreation has developed. Released from long hours of toil, people in increasing numbers have turned eagerly to recreational activities as an important part of their daily routine. Sports and amusements during the nineteenth century were ordinarily for the privileged few and were seldom enjoyed by the rank and file of the people except on holidays and special occasions. The remarkable expansion of recreation during the first three decades of the twentieth century has come about in response to the more universal demand for pleasurable ways of spending the leisure that is now so widely available.

Closely associated with expanding leisure is the increasing capacity of a large proportion of the American public to make purchases beyond the mere necessities of life. While the general upward trend in money wages in this country during the past forty or fifty years has been in a considerable measure offset by higher prices of commodities, there can be no doubt of the wide prevalence of a higher standard of living during the last decade than at the opening of the

[5] President's Research Committee on Social Trends, *Recent Social Trends in the United States,* Chapter XVI.

present century.[6] The greater purchasing power of the American public is apparent not merely from recent studies of family budgets but from the extraordinary consumption of commodities formerly beyond the means of all except the higher income classes. One automobile for every 5.3 persons in the population and a radio in two-fifths of the families are facts indicative of a new scale of living unique in the history of the nation. It has been this financial surplus remaining after essential needs are met that has brought recreational activities within reach of so many people. Increased purchasing ability gave momentum to the recreation movement and made possible its recent expansion along so many varied lines. A significant aspect of modern recreation is the trend away from the more simple pleasures to activities that require considerable outlay for facilities and equipment for play. With few exceptions the most popular games and sports are those that make heavy drains upon family budgets. Modern recreation occupies a prominent place in the present high cost of living and could have developed in such an extensive manner only in a period when there was capacity to meet a rising tide of expenditures.

This building of an urbanized, industrial world in which leisure time activities found a congenial soil for development has been accompanied by a changing outlook on life with greater emphasis upon the values of play and recreation. The modern recreation movement began to go forward when play gained recognition as a means to healthful living and was no longer stigmatized as a form of idleness. The early years of this century saw not merely a marked decline in religious opposition to amusements but also the promotion of recreational programs by churches and other religious organizations. A new era in the history of recreation began when the government accepted responsibility for the provision of public recreational facilities. Of real

[6] *Ibid.*, consult this source for data concerning recent changes in standards of living.

significance also is the greater willingness of the public school to accept as one of its functions the training of children for the wise use of leisure. The idea that adults as well as children need suitable facilities for games and sports, which did not gain full support until the years immediately following the World War, is largely responsible for the extraordinarily rapid growth of outdoor athletic sports during the past decade. Even more recently the right of women to participate freely in outdoor games has become widely recognized and is already making necessary a further expansion of recreational facilities.

During the past thirty years the earlier prejudices against sports and amusements have been replaced by an almost equally intolerant belief in their value and necessity. Recreation has become so securely entrenched in the habits and folkways of the people that it is now a dominating force wielding strong influence in many directions. In the eager rush to secure more time for recreational activities, Sunday blue laws have been swept aside and the entire week-end has for large numbers of people been turned entirely over to the pursuit of pleasure. The growing interest in adult recreation has brought a new and powerful force into the struggle for shorter hours of labor. The opening of the doors of recreation to the mass of the people strengthens their determination to attain a standard of living that will include ample provision for the enjoyment of leisure. Cities have found it profitable to build up recreational facilities and give them wide publicity in their efforts to attract new industries and increase their population. So universal has become the interest in recreation that it has led to the building up of huge enterprises reaching out into many fields of business and industry. The manufacture and sale of sporting goods, the furnishing of amusements on a commercial basis, and the vast army of coaches, play directors, professional sportsmen, sport writers, and others who make their living within the field of recreation are powerful forces that have been called into being by the insatiable desire for play and amusement. The direction this whole movement is taking is a matter deserving of serious study. In the following chapters an effort is made to indicate some of the more important changes during recent years in modern American recreation in order to make clear its present status and to throw light if possible on probable trends in the future.

Chapter II

DEVELOPMENT OF URBAN PLAYGROUNDS AND PARKS

WHILE the modern recreation movement sends its roots deep into the remote past and is the product of a large variety of factors and forces, any attempt to describe and interpret its course of development in America may very properly begin with the establishment of children's playgrounds and the gradual transformation of municipal parks into public recreation areas equipped with play facilities for both young and old. It was the lack of suitable opportunities for the play of children living in the congested portions of large cities that stimulated early efforts in the field of public recreation. The initial impetus of this new movement came from social and civic workers who provided funds for the establishment of the first public playgrounds and began building up a public opinion favorable to governmental support and direction of public recreational facilities.

One of the first landmarks of this play movement was the construction in 1886 by a private organization in Boston of a few sand gardens for children of kindergarten age. A few years later the park department of this same city built the Charlesbank Outdoor Gymnasium. In 1889 a few public tennis courts were provided in Washington and Jackson parks in Chicago and at about the same time permission was given to play baseball in these parks. The New York Society for Parks and Playgrounds was incorporated in 1890 but because of lack of public interest little was accomplished until a few years later. According to the 1907 Year Book of the Playground Association of America (now the National Recreation Association), public playgrounds were in operation in 11 cities prior to 1900. While their information was not complete, it is quite clear that this new movement had made very little headway before the opening of the present century.

Growth of Public Playgrounds.[1]—During the past two decades there has been a fairly rapid increase in the number of cities reporting public playgrounds. The best available

TABLE 1.—NUMBER OF CITIES REPORTING PUBLIC PLAYGROUNDS, BY GEOGRAPHICAL DIVISIONS AND CLASSES OF CITIES, 1910, 1920, 1930[a]

Geographical division	1910		1920		1930		Per cent of increase 1920–1930
	Number of cities reporting playgrounds	Per cent of all cities with playgrounds	Number of cities reporting playgrounds	Per cent of all cities with playgrounds	Number of cities reporting playgrounds	Per cent of all cities with playgrounds	
United States.......	180	7.5	428	15.4	695	22.0	62.6
New England.......	44	12.2	92	31.5	123	53.0	33.7
Middle Atlantic.....	60	12.0	131	21.7	178	24.8	35.8
East North Central	27	5.2	89	15.2	157	23.9	65.1
West North Central	14	5.0	32	9.9	51	14.5	59.4
South Atlantic......	11	5.2	34	12.5	3	18.5	85.3
East South Central	4	3.2	10	5.9	18	9.3	80.0
West South Central	2	1.1	6	2.3	32	9.9	433.3
Mountain.........	2	2.1	11	9.4	21	16.2	90.9
Pacific...........	16	13.9	23	13.9	52	23.5	126.1
Classes of cities							
All cities	180	7.5	428	15.4	695	22.0	62.6
2,500– 5,000.....	1	.....	26	2.0	47	3.5	80.7
5,000– 10,000....	12	1.9	83	11.5	113	13.3	36.1
10,000– 25,000....	51	13.7	122	26.5	238	39.3	95.0
25,000– 50,000....	41	34.2	78	54.5	124	67.0	58.9
50,000–100,000....	37	62.7	58	77.3	87	86.7	50.0
100,000–500,000....	30	71.4	50	87.7	70	88.8	40.0
500,000 and over....	8	100.0	11	91.7	13	100.0	18.2

a Compiled from the Year Books of the National Recreation Association and the volumes on Population of the U. S. Bureau of the Census for the years indicated.

[1] The term "public playground" as used in this discussion refers to all playgrounds open to the general public and includes those supported by private contributions as well as by school, park, or other governmental funds.

The data have been compiled from the Year Books of the National Recreation Association. The number of cities reporting playgrounds and the number of playgrounds differ somewhat from the figures given by the National Recreation Association. This is explained by the fact that in this report towns under 2,500 population are excluded, as well as all Canadian cities. Moreover, the totals given in the Year Books frequently include towns and small cities about which there is not sufficient information to justify their inclusion in the statistical tables used in the preparation of this report.

[15]

information indicates that the number of cities above 2,500 population maintaining playgrounds in 1910 was 180; in 1920 the number of playground cities had increased to 428, and in 1930 they numbered 695. In 1910 only 7.5 per

TABLE 2.—NUMBER OF PUBLIC PLAYGROUNDS BY GEOGRAPHICAL DIVISIONS AND CLASSES OF CITIES, 1910, 1920, 1930[a]

Geographical division	1910		1920		1930		Per cent of increase 1920–1930
	Number of playgrounds	Number per 100,000 urban population	Number of playgrounds	Number per 100,000 urban population	Number of playgrounds	Number per 100,000 urban population	
United States.......	1,300	3.0	4,139	7.6	7,240	10.5	74.9
New England.......	268	4.9	699	11.9	922	14.6	31.9
Middle Atlantic.....	617	4.5	1,395	8.3	2,225	10.9	59.5
East North Central	145	1.5	993	7.6	1,479	8.8	48.9
West North Central	70	1.8	296	6.2	475	8.5	60.5
South Atlantic......	92	2.9	288	6.6	703	12.3	144.1
East South Central	21	1.3	106	5.3	228	8.2	115.1
West South Central	8	0.4	60	2.0	270	6.1	350.0
Mountain.........	9	0.9	56	4.6	165	11.3	194.6
Pacific...........	70	2.9	246	7.0	773	14.0	214.2
Classes of cities							
All cities..........	1,300	3.0	4,139	7.6	7,240	10.5	74.9
2,500– 5,000....	1	0.02	31	0.7	103	2.2	232.3
5,000– 10,000....	20	0.5	175	4.0	259	4.4	48.0
10,000– 25,000....	95	1.7	350	5.0	955	10.5	172.9
25,000– 50,000....	131	3.2	449	8.9	834	13.0	85.7
50,000–100,000....	176	4.2	527	10.0	1,100	16.9	108.7
100,000–500,000....	307	3.5	1,044	9.4	1,761	11.4	68.7
500,000 and over....	570	0.0	1,563	9.6	2,228	10.7	42.5

[a] Compiled from the Year Books of the National Recreation Association and the volumes on Population of the U. S. Bureau of the Census for the years indicated.

cent of the cities above 2,500 population had playgrounds, while in 1930 this percentage had increased to 22. The greatest increase in the number of cities reporting playgrounds is found in the cities under 25,000 population. Since 1910 the number of playground cities of this class increased six times while those above 25,000 more than doubled (Table 1).

The number of playgrounds in cities above 2,500 population increased from 4,139 in 1920 to 7,240 in 1930, a gain of 74.9 per cent. Their growth has been more rapid than the urban population, for in 1910 there were 3 playgrounds per 100,000 urban population; in 1920, 7.6 per 100,000; and in 1930, 10.5 (Table 2). Two-thirds of all public playgrounds in operation in 1910 were in cities of 100,000 and above. Eight of the largest cities had 43.8 per cent of the play-

TABLE 3.—PER CENT DISTRIBUTION OF PLAYGROUNDS AND URBAN POPULATION, BY CLASSES OF CITIES, 1910, 1920, 1930[a]

Class of city	1910		1920		1930	
	Per cent urban population	Per cent playgrounds	Per cent urban population	Per cent playgrounds	Per cent urban population	Per cent playgrounds
All classes.............	100	100	100	100	100	100
2,500– 5,000........	9.6	.....	8.5	0.7	6.8	1.4
5,000– 10,000........	10.3	1.5	9.2	4.3	8.6	3.5
10,000– 25,000........	13.2	7.4	12.8	8.4	13.2	12.8
25,000– 50,000........	9.5	10.0	9.3	10.9	9.3	11.4
50,000–100,000........	9.8	13.6	9.7	12.7	9.4	15.4
100,000–500,000........	20.6	23.7	20.4	25.3	22.4	24.1
500,000 and over.......	27.0	43.8	30.1	37.7	30.3	31.4

[a] Compiled from the Year Books of the National Recreation Association and the Volumes on Population of the U. S. Bureau of the Census for the years indicated.

grounds at that time. The cities of 25,000 and under, on the other hand, made a slow beginning in the establishment of these facilities but showed consistent progress when once well started. In 1910 cities of this class had 8.9 per cent of the public playgrounds and in 1930 their percentage had about doubled. The cities of 100,000 population and above had 47.6 per cent of the total urban population and 67.5 per cent of the playgrounds in 1910, while 20 years later the percentage of playgrounds in cities of this class was only slightly greater than their percentage of the urban population (Table 3). In 1910 the cities of 500,000 and over had made the best provision for these recreational facilities considered from the point of view of the number per 100,000 urban population. In 1930 the first place had shifted to the medium sized cities, with the larger cities ranking second and the smaller cities ranking lowest as they had from the beginning of the recreation movement (Table 2).

The playground movement originated in the northeastern states (New England and Middle Atlantic) and gradually developed two other concentration areas, one in the East North Central states and the other on the Pacific coast in California. The northeastern states in 1910 and in 1920 had the largest number of playgrounds per 100,000 urban population, but in 1930 the Pacific coast states took first place. On the basis of proportion of urban population, all the geographical divisions except the two comprising the northeastern states had less than their quota in 1910. Twenty years later the only divisions that failed to attain their quota were the East and West North Central and the East and West South Central. One of the trends in the playground movement has been toward a more equitable distribution of playgrounds throughout the entire country. In 1910, 84.7 per cent of the playgrounds were found in the North while in 1930 this section of the country had only 70.4 per cent. The South in the meantime had increased its proportion of playgrounds from 9.2 per cent to 16.6 per cent, and the West from 6.1 per cent to 13.0 per cent. In 1930 both the North and the South closely approximated their quota of playgrounds while the West exceeded its quota by 3 per cent. Since 1920 the rate of increase in the number of playgrounds has been much greater in the South and West than in the North (Table 4).

Changes in Playground Construction and Activities.— When public playgrounds were first established, the equipment used consisted mostly of the type of apparatus common in the gymnasium. The playgrounds were usually small and this kind of equipment was especially appropriate because it accommodated large numbers in a small space. This traditional equipment is still widely used in modern playgrounds and is supplemented by very few new devices. Perhaps the greatest change is the declining use of such gymnastic apparatus as the buck, horse, and parallel bars. Swings, slides, travelling rings, giant strides, see-saws, and horizontal bars maintain their former popularity among children and are still recommended as standard

TABLE 4.—PER CENT DISTRIBUTION OF PLAYGROUNDS AND URBAN POPULATION, BY GEOGRAPHICAL DIVISIONS, 1910, 1920, 1930[a]

Section	Geographical division	1910		1920		1930	
		Per cent urban population	Per cent play-grounds	Per cent urban population	Per cent play-grounds	Per cent urban population	Per cent play-grounds
United States..............		100	100	100	100	100	100
North...	New England.......	12.8	20.6	10.8	16.9	9.1	12.7
	Middle Atlantic.....	32.2	47.5	30.7	33.7	29.6	30.7
	East North Central	22.6	11.2	24.0	24.1	24.4	20.4
	West North Central	9.1	5.4	8.7	7.2	8.1	6.6
	Total...........	76.7	84.7	74.2	81.9	71.2	70.4
South...	South Atlantic......	7.3	7.0	8.0	6.9	8.3	9.7
	East South Central	3.7	1.6	3.7	2.6	4.0	3.2
	West South Central	4.6	0.6	5.5	1.4	6.4	3.7
	Total...........	15.6	9.2	17.2	10.9	18.7	16.6
West....	Mountain.........	2.2	0.7	2.2	1.3	2.1	2.3
	Pacific............	5.6	5.4	6.4	5.9	8.0	10.7
	Total...........	7.8	6.1	8.6	7.2	10.1	13.0

[a] Compiled from the Year Books of the National Recreation Association and the Volumes on Population of the U. S. Bureau of the Census for the years indicated.

equipment for modern playgrounds. While the nature of the equipment has remained fundamentally the same, marked improvements have been made in construction and in the use of more durable materials which have resulted in greater safety and longer use.

Without doubt emphasis in playground construction has been turning rapidly in the direction of providing greater facilities for different kinds of games. Although the earlier playgrounds, when their size permitted, had some open space for such team games as baseball and football, little attention was given to the provision of facilities for a wide variety of sports. Emphasis was for the most part upon simple group games which required a minimum of equipment and very little in the way of specially constructed grounds. At the present time a well equipped playground or playfield frequently includes provision for such games and sports as field hockey, playground ball, volley ball, handball, soccer, roque, shuffle board, archery, horseshoes, clock golf, bowling, and tennis. In large playfields space is usually set aside for baseball and football; swimming pools and public bath ing facilities are also frequently provided. Other recent changes are better seating facilities for spectators, outdoor theaters, more satisfactory surfacing of play areas, greater attention to beautifying the grounds, and night illumination so that outdoor games may be played after dark.[2]

The recent expansion in facilities for physical activities and team games of many different kinds has been paralleled by increased emphasis upon a wide variety of special activities planned to meet the needs of different age groups. In 1910 only a small number of special playground activities formed a part of the regular program, but in 1930 they had become so numerous and diversified that they occupied a position of importance closely rivalling that held by athletic sports. Among the 40 special activities of playgrounds mentioned in the 1930 Year Book of the National Recreation Association, some of the more popular are art work, badge tests, circus, folk dancing, social dancing, handcraft, holiday celebrations, model aircraft, motion pictures, nature study, band concerts, community singing, pageants, and plays.

Play Supervision and Direction.—One of the important advances in the play movement has been the growing recognition of the value of leaders specially trained for the task of supervising and directing the playground activities. Largely through the influence of the National Recreation Association, the policy of providing trained

[2] George D. Butler, "Changes in Playground Design and Equipment," *Recreation*, 25: 95–96 (1931).

leaders is becoming more widely accepted. In 1910 the number of employed play leaders was 3,345 and twenty years later they had increased to 24,949. Between 1920 and 1930 the number of play leaders considerably more than doubled while the number of playgrounds increased 75 per cent. With a growing number of playgrounds open throughout the year, there is being built up a professional group of play leaders whose employment is no longer limited to summer vacations. In 1930 there were reported 1,399 playgrounds open throughout the year with 2,660 year round play supervisors. One of the activities of the National Recreation Association is the operation of a graduate training school in New York City for the preparation of playground workers. Supplementing the work of this school the Association conducts numerous institutes and short courses in different cities throughout the country. So widespread is the interest in this new type of employment that at least 140 colleges and universities offer vocational or pre-professional courses for recreation leaders. One of the important advances made during the past decade is the higher standards of play leadership and the wider recognition of the need of professional training for work of this kind.

Public School Playgrounds.—While traditionally the American public school has had as a part of its plant a school yard, it has only recently been considered essential to provide space sufficient for a playground planned to meet the needs of children of different ages. In 1908 it was estimated that the average play space per pupil was 10 to 20 square feet except in the newest schools where 30 square feet was regarded as a suitable standard.[3] When it is realized that with 30 square feet per child, one acre will provide a playground for 1,452 children, it is quite clear that school yards a generation ago were by no means well suited for recreational purposes.

During recent years there has been a marked tendency to secure more ample grounds when school buildings are

[3] *Ibid.*, pp. 95–96.

erected in new locations. In Rochester, New York, 12 recently purchased school sites contained an average of slightly more than 10 acres, approximately four times larger than the average site of schools previously built in that city. The standard set for school sites in Gary, Indiana, is 20 acres, ten of which are for the school building and playground and the remainder for a public park. In Winston-Salem, North Carolina, 10 schools erected since 1918 have a total of 265 acres of playground, athletic field, and park. These and other similar examples collected by the United States Office of Education seem to present satisfactory evidence of the trend toward more extensive school grounds.[4]

Nevertheless, the movement to provide more play space for children in school has proceeded somewhat slowly and unevenly. The small school yards of a generation ago still exist in large numbers and in some cases they have been seriously encroached upon by the erection of additional school buildings. In spite of all the progress that has been made, there are still many public schools without playgrounds. A survey of the status of physical education in city public schools published in 1929 pointed out that 20 per cent of the elementary schools in cities having a population of 30,000 to 100,000 had no playgrounds and that scarcely 50 per cent of the city high schools were provided with either playgrounds or athletic fields.[5] In 1928, 8 of the 48 elementary schools in Rochester, New York, had no usable play space and only 6 had playgrounds as large as two or three acres. The average play space was .74 acres or 44 square feet per child.[6] A similar survey of Indianapolis in 1929 revealed that the grade schools in that city had an average of only 59.5 square feet of play space for each

[4] Marie M. Ready, *School Playgrounds*, Pamphlet No. 10, U. S. Office of Education, 1930, pp. 36–38. See also *Proceedings* of the National Conference on Outdoor Recreation, Senate Document No. 117, 69th Congress, 1st Session, 1926, p. 104.

[5] Marie M. Ready, *Physical Education in City Public Schools*, Physical Education Series, No. 10, U. S. Bureau of Education, 1929, pp. 92–93, 99.

[6] C. B. Raitt, *A Survey of Recreational Facilities in Rochester, New York*, Rochester Bureau of Municipal Research, Rochester, New York, 1929, pp. 212–215.

school child.[7] These facts, which seem to be fairly typical of the situation in large cities, give some indication of the difficulties confronted by those who are endeavoring to develop a more adequate recreational program in the public schools. The new standards, which call for at least 5 acres for elementary schools, 10 acres for junior high schools, and 20 acres for senior high schools, are evidently being applied in many cities when new school sites are purchased, but cannot without almost prohibitive expense be put into effect in the case of old school plants located in congested districts where land values are high.

While legislation pertaining to the size of school playgrounds still lags behind the standards set up by competent authorities, considerable advance has been made in recent years. In 1930 there were at least 8 states that had passed laws which set up minimum requirements for school playgrounds. State boards of education in 20 states have adopted rules and regulations governing the size of school sites. The areas required by law or by regulations of state boards of education vary from one to six acres for elementary schools and from two to ten acres for high schools. Since 1925 about a dozen states have passed laws stating the maximum areas which school boards may take by condemnation proceedings, if necessary. In general these areas run from two to ten acres.[8] Because of the growing appreciation of the value of outdoor sports, this legislation is strongly supported by public opinion. There can be no doubt of the trend toward more adequate play space for public school children although the enlargement of school grounds procured during an earlier period will likely proceed slowly because of the expense involved.

The growing interest in recreation facilities for school children is apparent also in the progress made in providing more indoor play space for use during inclement weather. Either a gymnasium or an auditorium that can be used as

[7] E. T. Lies, *The Leisure of a People: A Report of a Recreation Survey of Indianapolis*, Indianapolis, 1929, p. 284.

[8] Marie M. Ready, *School Playgrounds*, Pamphlet No. 10, U. S. Office of Education, 1930, pp. 4–9.

a gymnasium is now regarded as standard equipment for new school buildings. Playrooms and less frequently swimming pools are also provided by some of the modern school plants. Unfortunately many thousands of old school buildings do not contain facilities for indoor play since they were built at a time when the need for recreational equipment was less keenly felt. In a recent study of the equipment for physical education in city public schools it was found that only 30 per cent of the elementary and high schools reporting in 410 cities had gymnasiums. Forty-eight per cent of the schools reported neither gymnasiums nor play rooms and presumably had made no provision for indoor games. Swimming pools were provided in one or more of the public schools in 23 per cent of the cities studied.[9] While provision for indoor recreation in the public schools is apparently on the increase, it seems to be lagging behind the development of grounds for outdoor games.

The more liberal provision for sports and games by public school authorities has made more apparent the need of supervision and direction of the children during their regular play periods, including the late afternoons and Saturdays when school is not in session. Especially is it becoming evident that there must be a breaking away from the old tradition that school grounds must be closed as soon as school is dismissed. The Department of Public Instruction in New Jersey reports a "tendency toward organizing activities for the pupils in the afternoon hours after the usual closing hour of school. This responsibility for the leisure-time of the child between the closing hour of school and the supper hour is being increasingly accepted by boards of education."[10] This tendency, however, is apparently not yet widespread. In a report issued by the United States Bureau of Education in 1929 it is stated that "few city school boards have provided for supervision of school yards during after-school hours. Nearly all of this work is voluntary as yet, and the most substantial supervision

[9] Marie M. Ready, *Physical Education in City Public Schools*, Physical Education Series, No. 10, U. S. Bureau of Education, 1929, p. 99.

[10] Information given in a letter under date of March 5, 1931.

provided has been gained through cooperation with the city playground and recreation departments."[11] One of the important recreational problems faced by many American communities is the devising of ways and means whereby children may make larger use of the play facilities of the school located in their neighborhood.

Expansion of Urban Parks.—The municipal park movement gained considerable headway in the larger cities during the closing decades of last century but popular interest in the development of parks in all cities, both large and small, is a product of the past twenty-five years. Prior to 1900 the idea prevailed that city parks should provide the kind of recreation that comes from quiet enjoyment of well landscaped, wooded areas. Park properties were first developed by horticultural experts and were not regarded as suitable places for active games and sports. The recent emphasis upon parks as playgrounds for the people, adults as well as children, initiated a new era in park design and construction

TABLE 5.—GROWTH OF MUNICIPAL PARKS, 1907, 1916, 1930

Size of city	1907[a]		1916[b]		1930[c]	
	Park acreage	Population per acre of parks	Park acreage	Population per acre of parks	Park acreage	Population per acre of parks
All cities.............	76,566.7	307.1	123,253.3	261.8	258,697.3	184.2
30,000–50,000.........	6,684.1	391.5	17,336.5	188.6	35,593.6	136.0
50,000–100,000........	10,515.9	312.7	19,488.0	227.8	36,049.5	180.0
100,000–300,000.......	26,208.6	173.2	36,677.4	191.5	99,599.7	108.5
300,000–500,000.......	10,073.1	288.3	20,089.2	202.1	29,715.6	157.7
500,000 and over.......	23,085.0	440.3	29,662.1	454.2	57,738.9	360.6

[a] Population estimate as given in U. S. Bureau of the Census, *General Statistics of Cities*, 1907, Table 1, p. 131. Park acreage, *ibid.*, Table 68, p. 500. I have used the total area of all public parks. The cities of population 300,000–500,000 and 500,000 and over are not separated in this volume, so it has been necessary to form these classes from data on individual cities.

[b] Population estimate as given in U. S. Bureau of the Census, *General Statistics of Cities*, 1916. Park acreage, *ibid.*, Table 3, p. 50. I have used figures for all "parks or other public grounds," both inside and outside of city limits. Population per acre of parks computed from these data.

[c] Computed from data given in U. S. Bureau of Labor Statistics, Bulletin No. 565, *Park Recreation Areas in the United States*, 1932.

[11] Marie M. Ready, *Physical Education in City Public Schools*, p. 99.

and is largely responsible for the rapid growth of the park movement during the past few decades.

Complete figures showing the recent growth of municipal park acreage are not available since the earlier surveys included only cities of 30,000 population and above (Table 5). The park acreage in cities of this class increased from 76,567 in 1907 to 258,697 in 1930, a gain of 237.8 per cent for this period, while the urban population increased approximately 65 per cent. In 1907 the population per acre of parks in these cities was 307.1; in 1916 it had decreased to 261.8; in 1925 it was 193.6; and in 1930 it had still further declined to 184.2.[12] The most rapid progress in park acreage since 1907 has been made by cities between 30,000 and 100,000 population. The cities between 100,000 and 300,000, which in 1907 ranked first in their park development based on population per acre of parks, still maintained in 1930 their first place judged by this standard.

Especially notable has been the growth of municipal parks since 1925. Two extensive park surveys made by the National Recreation Association and the United States Bureau of Labor Statistics in 1925–1926 and in 1930 show that in 534 cities from which reports were received in both surveys the total area set aside for parks increased from 201,445.7 to 279,257.8 acres, a gain of 38 per cent during this five year period. The trend toward greater park development in medium sized cities is shown by the fact that cities from 25,000 to 50,000 population doubled their park acreage and cities between 10,000 and 25,000 made a gain of 63 per cent. The park movement, however, is not making great headway in the smaller municipalities for in cities between 5,000 and 10,000 the increase in park acreage during this period was only 15 per cent. It is noteworthy also that the cities of 250,000 population and above did not greatly add to their park acreage between 1925 and 1930, their rate of increase ranging from 15 to 21 per cent for this period (Table 6).

[12] U. S. Bureau of the Census, *General Statistics of Cities*, 1907, 1916. U. S. Bureau of Labor Statistics, Bulletins No. 462, 565, *Park Recreation Areas in the United States*, 1928, 1932.

Since the 1930 park survey did not secure reports from all the cities and towns in the United States, no exact statement of the total acreage of municipal parks can be

TABLE 6.—PARK ACREAGE IN 534 CITIES, BY POPULATION GROUPS, 1925–1926, 1930[a]

Population group	Number of cities reporting	Total park acreage		Per cent of increase
		1925–1926	1930	
1,000,000 and over	5	31,089.7	37,684.91	21
500,000–1,000,000	8	17,299.7	20,010.60	15
250,000–500,000	21	47,932.1	56,550.18	18
100,000–250,000	54	43,805.6	66,633.60	52
50,000–100,000	85	25,305.3	33,622.65	32
25,000–50,000	103	17,993.9	37,775.43	109
10,000–25,000	174	12,701.6	20,815.52	63
5,000–10,000	84	5,317.8	6,159.57	15
Total	534	201,445.7	279,257.79	38

[a] U. S. Bureau of Labor Statistics, Bulletin No. 565, *Park Recreation Areas in the United States*, 1932.

TABLE 7.—ACREAGE OF MUNICIPALLY OWNED PARKS AND RECREATION SPACES, BY POPULATION GROUPS, 1930[a]

Population group	Number of cities and towns	Number reporting	Number of communities		Total park acreage
			Without parks	With parks	
1,000,000 and over	5	5	...	5	37,566.35
500,000–1,000,000	8	8	...	8	20,172.60
250,000–500,000	24	24	...	24	62,681.75
100,000–250,000	56	54	...	54	66,633.60
50,000–100,000	98	93	...	93	36,049.48
25,000–50,000	185	127	3	124	41,596.88
10,000–25,000	606	313	48	265	27,472.93[b]
5,000–10,000	851	448	123	325	16,631.28[c]
Total, all groups	1,833	1,072	174	898	308,804.87

[a] U. S. Bureau of Labor Statistics, Bulletin No. 565, *Park Recreation Areas in the United States*, 1932.
[b] Park acreage in 2 cities not reported.
[c] Park acreage in 3 cities not reported.

made. Eight hundred and ninety-eight cities above 5,000 population reported 308,805 acres of park property. The officials in 174 cities, nearly all of which were under 25,000 population, stated that they had no municipal parks (Table 7). In view of the fact that no reports were received from 761 cities, a conservative estimate of the total park area in American municipalities is at least 350,000 acres, which is one acre of park land for every 183 urban population. While practically all of the large cities have developed extensive park systems, they usually make a poor showing when ranked according to population per acre of parks.

TABLE 8.—CITIES OF 250,000 POPULATION OR ABOVE RANKED ACCORDING TO POPULATION PER ACRE OF MUNICIPAL PARKS, 1930[a]

City	Population per acre of parks	City	Population per acre of parks
1. Denver	23	21. Philadelphia	248
2. Dallas	42	22. Providence	252
3. Minneapolis	90	23. Boston	269
4. Houston	108	24. Columbus	269
5. Washington	114	25. St. Louis	279
6. Kansas City	116	26. Cleveland	285
7. St. Paul	119	27. New Orleans	285
8. Indianapolis	124	28. Birmingham	300
9. Louisville	127	29. Pittsburgh	358
10. Portland, Or	133	30. Buffalo	358
11. Cincinnati	142	31. Detroit	386
12. Seattle	145	32. Milwaukee	464
13. Rochester	176	33. New York	485
14. Atlanta	180	34. Akron	497
15. Toledo	182	35. Chicago	566
16. Memphis	186	36. Jersey City	3,495
17. San Francisco	221	37. Newark	11,403
18. Baltimore	231		
19. Los Angeles	235		
20. Oakland	246		

[a] Compiled from data given in U. S. Bureau of Labor Statistics, Bulletin No. 565, *Park Recreation Areas in the United States*, 1932.

Denver, Dallas, and Minneapolis are the only cities above 250,000 that have less than 100 people for each acre of park land. Only 16 of the 37 cities above 250,000 make a better showing than an acre of park land for each 200 population. No city above 500,000 reaches even this low standard (Table 8). From the point of view of park space in proportion to size of city, the highest standards have been reached by the cities from 25,000 and to 50,000 with one acre of park land for each 104 population. The cities that fall within the 100,000 to 250,000 population group rank second with one acre of parks for each 110 people (Table 9). It should be

TABLE 9.—AVERAGE NUMBER OF PERSONS PER ACRE OF MUNICIPAL PARKS, BY POPULATION GROUPS, 1930[a]

Population group	Number of cities reporting	Number of per- sons per acre of park	Population group	Number of cities reporting	Number of per- sons per acre of park
1,000,000 and over........	5	401	50,000–100,000..........	93	165[b]
500,000–1,000,000........	8	286	25,000–50,000...........	124	104[b]
250,000–500,000..........	24	127	10,000–25,000...........	263	139[b]
100,000–250,000..........	54	110	5,000–10,000............	322	129[b]

[a] U. S. Bureau of Labor Statistics, Bulletin No. 565, *Park Recreation Areas in the United States,* 1932.

[b] Estimated. The population of the median city reporting park acreage has been used in deter- mining the ratio of park acreage to population.

stated, however, that these figures include municipal parks located outside the city limits. Much of the advance made in enlarging park properties during recent years has consisted in the acquirement of outlying areas far distant from the congested residential districts and therefore contributing very little toward the solution of the problem of properly located neighborhood playfields. In 1930, 186 cities reported 381 municipal parks outside the city limits with a total acreage of 89,196. Phoenix leads with the largest out-of-the- city park of 14,640 acres. Denver has 44 such parks with a total of approximately 11,000 acres. While outlying parks are widely distributed among cities in 41 states, this type of park property is apparently more popular in Western cities. Nearly half of the cities reporting such parks are located west of the Mississippi river although this section of the country has only a few more than one-fourth of the cities above 5,000 population.

Municipal Park Recreation.—This extraordinary expan- sion of municipal parks has not merely made possible great advances in public recreation but in a large measure is a direct outgrowth of the demand for facilities for outdoor recreation. So strong has been the public pressure on park authorities to develop the recreational possibilities of park lands that it has brought about almost complete acceptance of the idea that a major function of parks is to provide recreation service. In a remarkably short period of time urban parks from one end of the country to the other have been equipped with a bewildering array of leisure-time facilities designed to meet the needs of both young and old. For the athletically inclined there are football gridirons, baseball diamonds, tennis courts, golf links, soccer fields, etc. Those who prefer less strenuous sports find opportunities to participate in croquet, roque, fly casting, archery, shuffleboard, trap-shooting, lawn bowling, and the like. The wide popularity of water sports has led to the construction of swimming pools, lagoons, and bathing beaches, and to provision for sailing, canoeing, motor boating, and other aquatic sports. Of great importance also are the park buildings used for social, educational, and recreational purposes. Examples of such structures are art galleries, band stands, club houses, conservatories, field houses, gymnasiums, moving picture booths, museums, outdoor theaters, dancing pavilions, and zoological gardens. Other facilities are ovens and tables for picnic parties, bridle paths, refreshment stands, summer camps, and shelter houses. A recent improvement is the installation of amplifying devices which make it possible for band concerts or other musical events to be heard by large numbers of people.

Along with this unparalleled development of park recreational facilities there has been an increasing tendency to build up a program of recreational activities designed to facilitate the widest possible use of the parks. This park program includes the promotion of competitive sports between organized groups, supervision of games of juveniles, dancing, theatricals, handcraft, pageantry, nature lore, and other diversions and instruction under personnel employed for this purpose. Well equipped park departments now provide a year-round program of activities which vary with the seasons and cover such a wide range that it is possible for all to find congenial recreation. Many of these recreational facilities are provided by the park authorities free of charge but it is becoming increasingly customary to charge small fees for certain forms of recreation and thus derive sufficient revenue to make them at least partially self-supporting. Fees are frequently charged for boats and canoes, tennis, golf, art museums, zoological gardens, swimming pools, camps, and dancing pavilions.

County Parks.—Municipal park systems in some sections of the country are being supplemented by parks established and maintained by county authorities. For the most part this movement has proceeded most vigorously in counties located in metropolitan regions and owes its chief impetus to the urgent demand for wider recreational facilities for city people. During the past decade county governments have shown an increasing willingness to follow the precedent set by a few of the urban counties and as a result there were, in 1930, 74 counties located in 20 states that maintain parks totaling 108,484 acres.[13]

The recent growth of interest in county parks is shown by the fact that prior to 1915 only 6 counties had made a beginning in this direction. In 1926, when the first attempt was made to collect complete information about county parks, 31 counties were reported as maintaining facilities of this kind.[14] Four years later the number of counties that had established parks had more than doubled. Popular support of the county park movement has by no means proceeded uniformly throughout the country. More than half of the counties maintaining parks and 80 per cent of the park acreage are found in six Northern states. Michigan and California stand first among the states in the number of counties having parks while Illinois and New York lead in county park acreage (Table 10).

[13] U. S. Bureau of Labor Statistics, Bulletin No. 565, *Park Recreation Areas in the United States*, 1932.
[14] U. S. Bureau of Labor Statistics, Bulletin No. 462, *Park Recreation Areas in the United States*, 1928.

TABLE 10.—Number of Counties with Parks, and Number and Acreage of County Parks, by States, 1930[a]

State	Number of counties with parks	Number of county parks	Total acreage of county parks
Northern states........	44	299	91,767
New York....................	4	32	22,959
New Jersey...................	6	58	9,988
Pennsylvania.................	1	2	4,010
Ohio........................	3	16	11,665
Indiana.....................	1	1	181
Illinois....................	6	87	36,236
Michigan....................	16	71	3,635
Wisconsin...................	7	32	3,093
Southern states..............	6	17	2,385
North Carolina..............	3	5	225
Georgia.....................	1	10	60
Florida.....................	2	2	2,100
Western states...............	24	99	14,332
Minnesota...................	2	3	227
North Dakota................	1	1	40
Iowa........................	1	3	80
Missouri....................	1	4	77
Texas.......................	2	6	286
Colorado....................	1	1	100
Wyoming.....................	1	2	80
California..................	12	74	13,070
Washington..................	3	5	372
Total.......................	74	415	108,484

[a] Compiled from U. S. Bureau of Labor Statistics, Bulletin No. 565, *Park Recreation Areas in the United States*, 1932.

Among the different types of county parks that have been established, the most important are the small park located near a large city and equipped as a place for games and sports; the large reservation some distance from the city and designed to preserve scenic areas and make them available for picnicking and camping; the parkway which provides broad and well surfaced driveways connecting places of special interest; and the rural park maintained by sparsely settled counties as a recreation center for rural people. More than half of the county parks are small in size, having 100 acres or less, but the large reservations account for the majority of the park acreage. Almost two-thirds of the total area of county parks is found in parks of 1,000 acres or more.[15]

Many of the county parks, because of their recent development and lack of funds, have lagged behind municipal parks in providing recreational facilities. In some places, however, considerable progress has been made in meeting the popular demand that they be equipped for outdoor recreation. The Union County park system in New Jersey provided in 1929 twenty-seven different types of recreational facilities which were enjoyed that year by more than two and a half million people. The Westchester County park system near New York City has during the past nine years had a phenomenal development and is now one of the important playgrounds for the New York metropolitan region. The Cook County Forest Preserves near Chicago have an area of 33,000 acres and in 1930 had an attendance of 15,000,000 people.

The county park movement is too recent a development to make possible any accurate statement concerning its future growth. While rapid progress has been made during the past decade, it must be remembered that as yet scarcely 2 per cent of the counties throughout the country have made a beginning in the development of park lands. This movement has attained its greatest success in counties located in metropolitan regions or in those having within their borders cities of 100,000 or more people. Less than one-third of the counties that have established parks may be regarded as distinctively rural. The movement has gained its first impetus from urban patterns and further advances are most likely to be made in counties where there is large urban influence.

[15] National Recreation Association, *County Parks*, New York, 1930, p. 50.

CHAPTER III

RECREATION AND OUTDOOR LIFE

ONE of the significant trends in modern recreation is the increasing demand for great open spaces set apart for the enjoyment of those outdoor diversions which have become so eagerly sought as means of escape from the noise and confusion of urban life. It has already been pointed out in the previous chapter how urban park systems are expanding beyond the city limits and are being supplemented by large park areas under control of county authorities. With the improvement of means of travel people are finding it possible to go even farther afield in their search for recreation and readily travel long distances during week-ends and vacations to places of scenic interest where their favorite forms of outdoor life may be enjoyed. This has brought about within recent years a wider use of national parks and forests and has led in some sections of the country to the establishment of state parks which are already playing an important role in modern recreation. Picnicking and camping, hiking and mountain climbing, hunting and fishing, sailing and motor boating, swimming at a bathing beach, and similar pastimes are diversions that possess a wide appeal. To some extent fortunately situated cities can provide opportunities for some of these types of recreation but for the most part they can be enjoyed best in the more remote places apart from urban crowds.

State Parks and Forests.—State parks and forests have been a development of the past fifty years and public interest in them did not gain much momentum until the opening of the present century. The past decade has been the period of most rapid expansion of this movement. Since 1920 more than two-thirds of existing state parks and forests have been established and the majority of the state governments have adopted the policy of setting aside state lands for outdoor recreational use.

State parks were first advocated for the purpose of preserving historical sites to which a sentimental interest was attached, such as the battlefields of the Revolution and the Civil War. This movement was strengthened by a growing interest in the preservation of places famous for their natural scenic beauty. Two of the first state parks of this latter kind were the Yosemite (1875) and Niagara Falls (1885). Efforts of the state governments to preserve forest land began with New York's prohibition of further sale of the Adirondack forest and the creation of a State Forest Commission (1885). Pennsylvania made its first purchase of forest lands in 1898. A few other states began to establish forest preserves but the movement made very little headway prior to the White House Conference on the Conservation of Natural Resources in 1908.[1]

Popular interest in the establishment of state parks and forests arose with the increased use of the automobile and the building of highways which made these places easily accessible to larger numbers of people. Parks and forests which had been thought of as places of scenic interest or as refuges for wild life began to be valued for their recreational uses. Camp sites and accommodations for tourists were developed and the growing interest in outdoor life strengthened the demand for a larger number of facilities of this kind. It was urged that since the national parks were for the most part located in the western states where they were convenient only to a small number of people, there should be acquired state parks and forests that would provide similar opportunities for camping and other outdoor diversions for people living in all sections of the country. The development of state lands for this purpose first gained headway in the eastern and north central states, then on the Pacific coast, and is now beginning to make progress in the southern and mountain states.

[1] Raymond H. Torrey, *State Parks and Recreational Uses of State Forests*, National Conference on State Parks, Inc., Washington, 1926, pp. 19–24.

In 1928 the state parks and forests numbered 563 with a total area of approximately four and one-half million acres. By far the greatest expansion of these state owned lands has occurred in the northeast and more especially in New York, where more than half of the acreage is located (Table 11).

TABLE 11.—NUMBER AND ACREAGE OF STATE PARKS AND STATE FORESTS, BY GEOGRAPHICAL DIVISIONS, 1928[a]

Geographical division	State parks		State forests		Total parks and forests	
	Number	Acreage	Number	Acreage	Number	Acreage
United States..........	351	2,729,840	212	1,750,195	563	4,480,035
New England..........	43	28,718	129	196,186	172	224,904
Middle Atlantic........	66	2,281,509	30	154,831	96	2,436,340
East North Central.....	97	158,540	20	149,774	117	308,314
West North Central....	80	215,410	3	456,000	83	671,410
South Atlantic.........	4	5,640	9	19,951	13	25,591
East South Central.....	4	2,224	5	3,734	9	5,958
West South Central.....	1	1,128	4	11,564	5	12,692
Mountain..............	5	7,431	9	694,566	14	701,997
Pacific................	51	27,326	3	63,589	54	90,915

[a] Compiled from Beatrice W. Nelson, *State Recreation*, National Conference on State Parks, Inc., Washington, 1928, pp. 430–431.

The least advance has been made in the southern states, which have less than one per cent of the total area of state parks and forests. Since 1920 the number of state parks and forests have increased 70 per cent while the acreage has increased only 40 per cent, thus indicating a trend toward the acquirement of areas of smaller size than was customary in earlier years. The most marked change, however, has been their development for popular use. Camp sites are being provided with proper sanitation and water supply. Cabins, hunting lodges, and hotels are being built for the convenience of tourists. Opportunities are offered in these parks for camping, hiking, boating, bathing, hunting, fishing, and winter sports. In some states a small charge is made to visitors which is used for the upkeep and further improvement of the parks. There is a growing tendency to develop these service areas in limited sections of the parks and leave the remainder a wilderness preserved in its natural condition.

While state parks and forests have been a recent development, the location of many of them near large metropolitan centers has caused them to have far more visitors than do many of the national parks. According to the National Association of State Parks, one park area in New York was visited by 13,000,000 people in 1930. Park areas in Michigan were visited during the same year by 8,900,000 people; in Connecticut by 1,428,514; and in Indiana by 950,000. The estimate made by this Association of the total number of visitors to state parks in 1930 was between forty and forty-five million people.[2]

National Parks.—In 1931 there were 22 national parks located in 16 states with one each in Alaska and Hawaii. They are by no means equally distributed throughout the country, the majority being in the mountain and Pacific coast states. Only two are east of the Mississippi River with two additional eastern sites approved by Congress in 1926 for development as soon as lands for this purpose have been donated. These national parks vary in size from Carlsbad Caverns, which has an area of 1.12 square miles, to the Yellowstone with an area of 3,426 square miles. The total area of the national park system is 12,542 square miles or 8,027,216 acres.[3] While the first national park was created as early as 1872, prior to 1900 only five had been established. Between 1900 and 1920 thirteen national parks were acquired. During the past decade four more were added with two other sites designated for future development.[4]

Prior to the World War the national parks were valued primarily for their scenic beauty and in general were not easy of access with the means of travel then available. In 1915 the visitors to the 13 national parks then in existence

[2] Report of Special Committee on Conservation of Wild Life Resources, *Wild Life Conservation*, Senate Document No. 1329, 71st Congress, 3rd Session, 1931, p. 5.

[3] *Annual Report of National Park Service*, 1931.

[4] The proposed new parks are Shenandoah Valley and Mammoth Cave.

numbered 334,799. The growing conception of these parks as the people's playgrounds, together with their greater accessibility made possible by automobiles and improved roads, greatly increased their popularity. By 1920 the annual number of visitors had increased to 919,504, and in 1931 they numbered 3,152,845. Twenty years ago Hot Springs national park, famous as a health resort because of its mineral springs, led in the number of visitors and was the only park with an attendance of more than 100,000 a year. Following the World War, Rocky Mountain national park took the lead, and in 1931 the most popular parks ranked according to the number of visitors were as follows: Yosemite, Platt, Mount Rainier, Rocky Mountain, Yellowstone, Crater Lake, Acadia, Grand Canyon, Great Smoky Mountains, Hot Springs, Sequoia, and Hawaii. Although few of these parks are located within easy reach of large centers of population, each park has more than 100,000 annual visitors and Yosemite attracts nearly half a million (Table 12). This extraordinary popularity of the national parks has been brought about chiefly by better means of travel within as well as outside the parks and by the efforts of the National Park Service to provide accommodations for tourists together with recreational facilities. The annual appropriations for the administration and improvement of the national park system have increased from approximately one million to twelve million dollars during the past ten years. For roads and trails within these parks the expenditures since 1925 amount to $22,500,000.

Whether the strong upward trend during the past decade in the development and wider use of the national parks will continue, it is difficult to predict. The present need for economy in governmental expenditures may hamper the carrying out of further plans for their expansion. It is noteworthy, however, that the visitors to the national parks have continued to increase during the financial depression, the gain being greater between 1929–1931 than during the two preceding years. Since the national parks are not protected by constitutional provision, efforts are constantly being made to get control of such portions of them as would be profitable for private exploitation. On the other hand, influential groups are taking measures to safeguard the future of the national parks and to establish new ones in areas suitable for this purpose. The growing demand for

TABLE 12.—NUMBER OF VISITORS TO NATIONAL PARKS, 1910–1931[a]

Name of park	1910	1920	1930	1931
Acadia (Maine)	[b]	66,500	154,734	162,238
Bryce Canyon (Utah)	[b]	[b]	35,982	41,572
Carlsbad Caverns (New Mexico)	[b]	[b]	90,104	81,275
Crater Lake (Oregon)	5,000	20,135	157,693	170,284
General Grant (California)	1,178	19,661	43,547	51,995
Glacier (Montana)	[b]	22,449	73,776	63,497
Grand Canyon (Arizona)	[b]	67,315	172,763	156,964
Grand Teton (Wyoming)	[b]	[b]	60,000	62,000
Great Smoky Mountains (North Carolina, Tennessee)	[b]	[b]	[b]	154,000
Hawaii (Hawaii)	[b]	[b]	89,578	124,932
Hot Springs (Arkansas)	120,000	162,850	167,062	153,394
Lassen Volcano (California)	[b]	2,000	31,755	56,833
Mesa Verde (Colorado)	250	2,890	16,656	18,003
Mount McKinley (Alaska)	[b]	[b]	951	771
Mount Rainier (Washington)	8,000	56,491	265,620	293,562
Platt (Oklahoma)	25,000	27,023	178,188	325,000
Rocky Mountain (Colorado)	[b]	240,966	255,874	265,663
Sequoia (California)	2,407	31,508	129,221	143,573
Sullys Hill (North Dakota)	190	9,341	21,293	[c]
Wind Cave (South Dakota)	3,387	38,000	88,000	85,000
Yellowstone (Wyoming)	19,575	79,777	227,901	221,248
Yosemite (California)	13,619	68,906	458,566	461,855
Zion (Utah)	[b]	3,692	55,297	59,186
Grand total	198,606	919,504	2,774,561	3,152,845

[a] Compiled from annual reports of the National Park Service.

[b] Park not established at this date.

[c] Discontinued as a national park early in 1931 and now administered as a game preserve by the Department of Agriculture.

wider facilities for outdoor life is apparently building up a public opinion favorable to setting aside for public use much more mountain land than is now available in the existing national parks. The older idea that national parks should be established only in places that possess unique features of scenic interest may be compelled to give way to a conception of their utility for purposes of outdoor recreation. The trend seems to be in the direction of preserving for future park development as many sites as may be practicable in the various sections of the country so that more people can have access to places where outdoor life may be enjoyed.

National Forests.—The National Forests, formerly known as the Forest Reserves, were set aside from other public lands by presidential proclamations issued for the most part during the administrations of Cleveland, McKinley, and Roosevelt. It was hoped that through federal administration of these lands the forests would not be exploited ruthlessly by private interests, that they could be more adequately protected from fire hazards, and that reforestation could be carried on in an extensive manner. While the national forests were a direct outgrowth of a national policy of conservation, it was never the intention of the government to preserve these forests in their original state as it does the national parks, but rather to regulate the sale of timber to private companies so that the output would be continuous, thus giving stability to the lumber industry and to the communities dependent upon it. The amount of timber cutting going on in the national forests has recently amounted to more than a billion board feet a year and has doubled since 1920.[5] An extensive program of reforestation is constantly going on under the direction of the Forest Service but because of a lack of funds it has not been possible to keep pace with losses by forest fires and timber sales.

The national forests covered in 1931 a gross area of 185,251,582 acres and are located in 26 states, 10 of which are east of the Mississippi River. Since they offer almost unlimited opportunities for hunting, fishing, and camping, they have become very popular as summer recreation grounds among those who wish to spend some time amid natural surroundings. The Forest Service permits the public to use these forests without charge, the only restrictions being those designed to decrease fire hazards and avoid the danger of water pollution. Nearly 1,750 camp grounds have been set aside and at least partially equipped with

[5] *Report of the Forester*, 1930, p. 30.

facilities essential to public health and convenience. Provision has been made for certain public service utilities such as stores, garages, and inns located at strategic points. As a result of this liberal policy concerning the recreational use of the forests, there has been an enormous increase in the number of visitors each year. In 1917, the first year that a systematic effort was made to estimate the number of visitors, 3,160,000 people made use of the forests for some form of outdoor recreation. During the past decade visitors have increased more than six times, from 4,832,671 in 1920 to 31,904,515 in 1930 (Table 13). The recent tendency seems to be to use these forests for brief outings and sight seeing trips, for during the past five years the number of hotel and resort guests and campers slightly declined while the transient tourists and picnickers more than doubled. Seventy-eight per cent of all the visitors in 1930 were classified as transient tourists.

TABLE 13.—VISITORS TO THE NATIONAL FORESTS, 1917–1930[a]

Year	Number of visitors	Year	Number of visitors
1917	3,160,000	1924	11,394,366
1918	3,322,565	1925	15,279,730
1919	3,964,344	1926	17,112,024
1920	4,832,671	1927	18,523,888
1921	5,433,420	1928	23,008,997
1922	6,172,942	1929	31,758,231
1923	10,543,893	1930	31,904,515

[a] From memorandum furnished by the Forest Service.

The use of the national forests by the public is still further facilitated by the policy of issuing special use permits for the erection of summer homes, resorts, hotels, or other structures for recreational purposes. The annual rental charges are low and many people take advantage of this opportunity to secure sites for summer cottages at small expense. At the close of 1930 there were 1,201 hotels, resorts, or summer camps and 10,770 summer homes under permit on national forest lands. In the national forests in California there are 15 recreation camps maintained by municipalities of that state. In addition to these the Forest Service has granted free permits for summer camps to a number of organizations such as the Boy Scouts, Girl Scouts, and the Young Men's Christian Association.

While the national forests were established as a part of the policy of conservation of natural resources, there has arisen a demand that they be preserved in so far as it is practicable as places for the enjoyment of camping and outdoor life. The attractiveness of the forests from the point of view of outdoor recreation depends to a great degree upon their primeval state. This suggests the advisability of placing greater restrictions upon the sale of timber from these areas as well as a more vigorous policy of reforestation. An important policy recently adopted by the Forest Service calls for the setting aside of so-called primitive areas in each of the forest regions so that extensive forests of the wilderness type will always be available for those who wish to enjoy camp life under natural conditions. Perhaps the growing interest in the use of the forests for recreational purposes may before it is too late bring about a much more extensive application of this policy than is now contemplated.

Camps and Camping.—So popular has camping become during the past two decades that it is now organized on a commercial basis, supported by private philanthropy, and directly fostered by municipal, state, and federal authorities. This urge to participate in camp life has been facilitated by the automobile and improved highways which have made remote and sparsely settled places fairly easily accessible to large numbers of people.

Organized summer camps for children were first established in the seventies and eighties of last century but made very little headway prior to 1900. According to Porter Sargent's Manual of Summer Camps, during the first decade of the present century there were 102 such camps, 88 per cent of which were located in the northeastern states. The first camps for boys and girls were established in New England, and as late as 1920 the majority were located in this region. During the past decade organized camps of this kind have spread more widely so that in 1930 only one-fourth of the total were located in New England. Between 1910 and 1920 the camp movement grew in popularity but its period of most rapid growth has been during the past decade.

These private camps operated on a commercial basis have for the most part been located in those states where the scenery and climate are best suited for outdoor life in the summer. Camps of this type are well equipped, have competent personnel, and provide an interesting and varied round of activities. While they are primarily recreational in nature, some opportunities for serious study are ordinarily arranged for those who desire it. Those more permanently organized now number considerably more than one thousand and their period of operation extends throughout most of the summer season. Camps of this kind usually cater to the upper middle and wealthier classes and are coming to be relied upon as a satisfactory means of providing wholesome recreation for children during the summer months when school is not in session.

The organized camp movement has made its greatest advance under the auspices of character building and other welfare organizations which now make camping a regular feature of their programs. According to figures given out by national organizations,[6] during the year 1929 there were 7,368 organized camps which accommodated 1,142,500 campers. These camps are usually operated on a cost basis with expenditures per capita kept at a low figure. For the benefit of those unable to bear the expense of camp life, some organizations maintain free camps or contribute funds to be expended in giving camp privileges to people of this class. Among the national organizations that have placed great emphasis upon camping is the Boy Scouts of America. In 1929 their national headquarters reported 539 camps with 114,057 scouts in attendance, an increase of 15 per cent over the preceding year. Purchase of permanent

[6] Article on "Camping," *Encyclopaedia of the Social Sciences*, Vol. 3: 169.

camp sites is a part of the policy of the organization and already more than four million dollars have been expended for this purpose.[7] Other agencies and organizations that conduct summer camps are the Girl Scouts, Camp Fire Girls, Young Men's Christian Association, Young Women's Christian Association, Jewish Welfare Board, Salvation Army, and many other religious and welfare groups.

The growth of camping is especially apparent in the recent efforts of municipal, county, state, and national governments to provide camping facilities on government owned lands. In 1928 one hundred cities maintained municipal camps, usually located at a considerable distance from the city at suitable sites with transportation frequently provided by the municipality.[8] The city of Los Angeles operated in 1930 six camps, four on mountain lands owned by the National Forest Service and two in an outlying park. Transportation to the mountain camps, located from 75 to 335 miles from the city, is arranged for campers who do not drive their own cars. The camp equipment consists of cabins, recreation lodge, community dining hall, athletic field, swimming pool, outdoor fireplace, and miscellaneous recreational facilities. The charges are kept as nearly as possible on a cost basis. The mountain camps are open to all but during the crowded season preference is given to citizens of Los Angeles. The boys' and girls' camps located in one of the city parks are operated every day during the summer months and during week-ends the remainder of the year. Meals, sleeping accommodations, and all recreational facilities and supervision are provided at the low cost of one dollar per day for each camper.[9]

The camp movement is also being promoted by the county and state park authorities who have widely adopted the policy of establishing and equipping camp sites on these government lands. By far the greatest advance made by governmental authorities in facilitating camping has been by the National Park Service. All the national parks main-

[7] *20th Annual Report of Boy Scouts of America*, 1929, p. 158.
[8] *Social Work Yearbook*, 1929, p. 447.
[9] Los Angeles Recreation Department, *Annual Report*, 1930.

tain free camp grounds equipped more or less completely for the use of park visitors. In 17 of the national parks for which reports of camping are available, the public camps in 1931 were used by more than 750,000 people who constituted nearly 30 per cent of the total visitors to those parks. Of the visitors to the national forests who remain longer than one day, the campers outnumber those who stay at hotels and resorts. During 1930 the National Forest Service reported 1,980,736 campers.[10] In view of the growing popularity of camping a conservative estimate of the annual number of campers on national reservations at the present time would be no less than 3,000,000.

The modern trend toward camping can also be seen in the development of the auto roadside camp for the benefit of those who travel long distances by automobile.[11] When automobiles first came into use for touring, those who did not wish to stop at hotels carried their own camp equipment and made their camp wherever suitable sites could be found. This demand for camp sites caused some municipal authorities to permit tourists to camp in the more secluded sections of public parks. Then commercial organizations, anxious to attract tourists, began to develop camping places furnished with water, sanitary facilities, and other conveniences. At first these motor camps were free and those promoting them relied upon sales to tourists to reimburse them for their outlay. Gradually sentiment developed in favor of a fixed charge for camping facilities but as late as 1925 only 20 per cent of the camps listed by the American Automobile Association reported some form of charge. During the past five years the trend has been in the direction of providing more adequate accommodations for which a suitable charge is made.

Following the World War well equipped municipal auto camps were built by many of the cities located in sections of the country attractive to tourists or along routes of travel traversed by tourists on their way to summer or winter

[10] Annual Reports of the National Park Service and the Forest Service.

[11] Cf. the monograph in this series entitled *Communication Agencies and Social Life.*

resorts. Examples of the more elaborate types of municipal camps are Bacon Park, West Palm Beach, Florida, and Campe Grande, El Paso, Texas. In such camps different grades of living accommodations can be secured as well as a wide variety of services, all provided at reasonable prices. According to the Official Camping and Camp Site Manual of the American Automobile Association issued in 1925, 50 per cent of the 1,400 auto camps for which information was secured were operated by municipalities. During the past few years municipal camps have been declining in numbers and importance and their place is being taken by roadside camps run by private enterprise. These privately operated camps are seen at their best in the western states where they are located along all the main travelled highways at frequent intervals. In the East and South they are less common but are increasing each year.

No accurate information is available concerning the total number of auto road camps. The Civic Development Department of the United States Department of Commerce estimated that there were 1,000 such camps in 1922. In a report issued four years later by this same organization it was stated that they numbered at least 2,000. The 1930 edition of the Recreational Directory of the American Automobile Association contains a descriptive list of 1,786 auto camps. This list includes only those from which information could be secured about their accommodations and necessarily excludes many of the smaller and less well equipped camps. Five thousand would be a very conservative estimate of the total number of auto camps throughout the country and they are apparently increasing by the hundreds each year.

The recent trend in auto road camps is strongly in the direction of more elaborate living accommodations. In the beginning of their development they provided little more than shelter and sanitary conveniences, and those who patronized them experienced the pleasures and hardships of camp life. Apparently they are now becoming more like roadside hotels in which camping will play a declining role.

The transformation of the crude roadside camp into attractively furnished cabins seems to be characteristic of the camping movement as a whole. As camping becomes more popular, the accommodations are improved so as to attract more people. It is becoming quite common for fishing and hunting lodges and various other types of camps to list among their attractions such things as electricity, steam heat, hot and cold showers, dining rooms, golf, tennis, dancing, and similar features. Outdoor life in the more remote places is being made more popular by approximating as closely as possible urban conditions. Real camp life of the traditional sort still exists in many places but the trend seems to be in the direction of a modified form of camping in which modern comforts and luxuries will play a more important part than was the case in the past.

Hunting and Fishing.—While comprehensive and adequate surveys of the game situation have not yet been made, there is general agreement among sportsmen and conservationists concerning the rapid decrease of wild life, especially in those sections of the country that are most thickly populated. The hordes of fishermen and hunters together with timber cutting, forest fires, water pollution, drainage, and the use of land for agricultural purposes have made inevitable a growing scarcity of game and are more and more limiting the opportunities for hunting and fishing which have furnished popular outdoor recreation to large numbers of people since colonial days.

According to the latest governmental reports, 6,903,017 hunting licenses and 5,318,104 fishing licenses were issued during the season 1929–1930 (Table 14). Since these figures include approximately 4,500,000 combination fishing and hunting licenses issued in a number of the states, a fair estimate of the total number of people licensed to engage in one or the other of these sports would be at least seven and a quarter million. Licenses, however, are not a complete measure of the extent of hunting and fishing since game laws are not always adequately enforced, and licenses are not usually required of those enjoying these sports on their own premises. The recent report of the Special Senate Committee on Conservation of Wild Life Resources estimated that 13,000,000 people in the United States either fished or hunted during the year 1929.[12]

TABLE 14.—NUMBER OF FISHING LICENSES ISSUED IN 1930 CLASSIFIED BY GEOGRAPHICAL DIVISIONS[a]

Geographical division	Number of licenses	Geographical division	Number of licenses
United States............	5,318,104	South Atlantic...........	406,549
		East South Central.......	60,628
New England............	381,146	West South Central......	169,511
Middle Atlantic..........	1,071,409	Mountain...............	440,855
East North Central.......	1,015,801	Pacific.................	520,914
West North Central.......	1,251,291		

[a] Compiled from U. S. Bureau of Fisheries, Document No. 1098, *Propagation and Distribution of Food Fishes*, 1930, pp. 1132–1133. The above figures include also combination hunting and fishing licenses.

Apparently there has been a considerable increase in the number of hunters and fishermen during recent years but it is impossible to make an exact statement of the amount of this increase. The Bureau of Biological Survey of the United States Department of Agriculture has a record of hunting licenses which includes combination hunting and fishing licenses since 1920 but reports of several states are lacking and some are obviously estimates. According to figures given out by this Bureau, the number of hunting licenses increased from 4,083,914 in 1920 to 6,903,017 in 1930, a gain of 69 per cent (Table 15). Similar records of fishing licenses, unfortunately, have not been assembled over a period of years. Some evidence of the growing vogue of this sport can be found in the recent increase in the manufacture of fishing apparatus. The value of fishing apparatus manufactured in 1927, the first year that this class of sporting goods was listed separately by the Census of Manufactures, amounted to $7,563,276.[13] In 1929 the

[12] *Wild Life Conservation*, Senate Document No. 1329, 71st Congress, 3rd Session, 1931, p. 4.

[13] While this amount includes fishing apparatus intended for commercial use as well as for sport, by far the largest share of this class of manufactured articles must be classified as sporting goods.

value of fishing apparatus manufactured during the year had increased to $8,572,607, a gain of 13.3 per cent during this two-year period.[14] Improved methods of transportation by both land and water have made remote fishing grounds more accessible than in the past and less time is consumed in going to and from fishing grounds. Fishing perhaps even more than hunting has continued to grow in popularity and is an eagerly sought leisure time activity of large numbers of people.

TABLE 15.—NUMBER OF HUNTING LICENSES ISSUED IN 1920 AND 1930, CLASSIFIED BY GEOGRAPHICAL DIVISIONS[a]

Geographical division	Number of licenses		Per cent increase
	1920	1930	
United States...................	4,083,914	6,903,017	69.0
New England...................	348,832	341,831	2.0 (decrease)
Middle Atlantic.................	846,024	1,428,068	68.8
East North Central..............	1,166,302	1,705,763	46.2
West North Central.............	422,730	1,180,657	179.0
South Atlantic..................	226,465	695,529	207.1
East South Central.............	100,806	198,707	97.1
West South Central.............	192,173	435,242	126.4
Mountain......................	323,838	408,121	26.0
Pacific........................	454,953	508,887	11.8
Alaska........................	....	214	

[a] Compiled from information furnished by the Bureau of Biological Survey, U. S. Department of Agriculture. The above figures include also combination hunting and fishing licenses.

While the increased participation in hunting and fishing cannot be measured accurately, it is quite clear that these sports continue to play a very important role in outdoor recreation. From the point of view of financial expenditures, hunting and fishing have become so widespread and involve such large outlays of money that they add very considerably to the recreation bill of the nation. The value of sporting firearms manufactured each year is much greater than that of golf goods and more fishing rods and reels are produced than tennis rackets. The Special Senate Committee on Conservation of Wild Life Resources estimated that three

[14] *United States Census of Manufactures,* 1927, 1929.

quarters of a billion dollars are expended each year in the purchase of ammunition and firearms for hunting, for fishing tackle, for canoes, tents, and equipment used in fishing and hunting, and for transportation to and from fishing and hunting grounds.[15]

So great has become the popular interest in these sports that the point is rapidly being reached where they can yield only diminishing returns to those who seek enjoyment in these forms of recreation. It is already being predicted that hunting and fishing will disappear as popular sports for the general public and that they will be limited to those able to hold memberships in exclusive clubs with resources sufficient to purchase fishing rights in lakes and rivers and to control their own game preserves. Such a decline in these traditional sports seems inevitable unless a well planned and comprehensive program of wild life conservation is put into effect. In many quarters recognition of this situation is leading to the enactment of more adequate game laws and their more effective enforcement. Besides the various state and federal departments that have responsibility for game preservation and conservation, there are more than 30 national organizations actively engaged in work of this kind. At the present time it is estimated[16] that the federal and state governments are expending annually about $12,000,000 for the conservation of the wild life resources in this country. Thus far this sum has proved to be inadequate and efforts are being made to develop a public opinion that will demand more liberal appropriations for this purpose.

Hiking and Mountain Climbing.—In spite of the widespread use of the automobile, walking as a form of recreation still proves attractive to many thousands of people. According to the Forest Service, 220,853 hikers visited the national forests during 1930. In New York City walking clubs have increased in number during the past ten years.

15 *Wild Life Conservation* Senate Document No. 1329, 71st Congress, 3rd Session, 1931, p. 5.
16 *Ibid.*, p. 6.

Trails have been built in the surrounding country by volunteer members of these clubs and the Palisades Interstate Park Commission has put up shelters for hikers along the trails in Bear Mountain Park.[17] Park and recreation departments in many of the large cities promote hiking as a part of their regular program of activities and sponsor week-end trips to neighboring places of interest. The Municipal Hiking Club of Minneapolis conducted in 1928 eighty-eight hikes with 4,187 participants. This hiking club, which has been in operation since 1920, carries on its activities both summer and winter and is an established feature of the recreational program of the city board of park commissioners.[18]

While hiking clubs, both public and private, can be found in all sections of the country, they enjoy their greatest popularity in places where mountain climbing can be participated in by their members. Among the best known clubs of this kind are the Appalachian and Green Mountain Clubs in the East, the Sierra Club of San Francisco, the Mazamas of Portland, Oregon, the Mountaineers of Seattle, and the Colorado Mountain Club of Denver. These clubs, nearly all of which are more than twenty-five years old, still continue to have a large membership and maintain a position of influence in outdoor recreation. Their members have done much to stimulate interest in mountain climbing and have frequently been leaders in the movement for a more adequate system of state and national parks and forests.

Aquatic Recreation.—Traditionally our waterways were regarded as aids to transportation and the water fronts of our cities have as a matter of course been turned over to commercial and industrial uses. In the early history of our country little attention was paid to the development of marine parks or to the possible utilization of the waterways and beaches for recreational purposes. Long before city planning got under way the waterways in cities were lined

[17] Lee F. Hanmer, *Public Recreation*, pp. 83–86, Regional Survey of New York and its Environs, Vol. 5, New York, 1928.

[18] *Playground and Recreation*, 24: 147 (1930).

with docks, warehouses, and manufacturing establishments and rarely was any shore land set aside for public use. With few exceptions the water front became the least attractive portion of cities and the amusements that became associated with it were often of a low commercial type that catered to the rougher element in the population.

The recent development of interest in outdoor life has brought with it a new appreciation of the recreational value of the waterways of the nation. A strong protest has arisen against the complete exploitation of water fronts by private interests and much progress has been made in developing attractive parks along the shores of rivers, lakes, and ocean. One of the notable accomplishments of this kind is the lake front parkway in Chicago which has been made possible by building up new land for miles along the shore of Lake Michigan, an enterprise that will eventually make available for public use almost the entire shore line of the city. This movement to beautify the water front and make it an area suitable for enjoyment by the public has become widespread in American cities but still lags behind what has been accomplished in Europe. The importance of this trend can hardly be exaggerated, for practically all of the large cities and hundreds of the smaller ones have had their sites originally determined by the presence of waterways of one kind or another and therefore can enjoy this recreational resource to the extent that it is developed.

The type of recreational use of our waterways that has made an especially wide appeal is the development of municipal beaches. The attendance at the bathing beaches in Chicago during the summer of 1930 was approximately 7,000,000. Since 1905 attendance at the bathing beaches in this city increased six times and between 1925 and 1930 the attendance doubled. Reports from 81 of the 218 cities that maintained bathing beaches in 1930 showed that the seasonal attendance for that year was 39,473,637, an average of nearly 500,000 per city. Not only are the bathing beaches becoming more crowded with people but new public beaches are being established each year by cities that possess suitable water front areas. Between 1923 and 1930 the number of cities above 2,500 reporting public bathing beaches increased from 127 to 218 while the number of beaches grew during this same period from 260 to 408.[19] Among the factors that have enhanced the popularity of municipal bathing beaches are the provision of field houses equipped with lockers, dressing rooms, and refreshment booths; the employment of life guards alert to prevent accidents; the promotion of water sports by the park authorities; and the transformation of the unwieldy bathing costumes of the past into a more simple swimming suit far better adapted to its purpose.

The further development of swimming and bathing as a sport is hampered by the pollution of many of the urban waterways by the discharge of oil from steamers and more frequently by dumping into them sewage, garbage, and other waste products. A federal law has been enacted providing for the limitation of the discharge of oil in coastal waters but this has not fully solved the problem. In some cities properly equipped sewage disposal plants have been constructed but this has proved to be expensive and it is difficult to develop a public opinion that will demand an improvement of this kind. The traditional custom of dumping the waste products of factories into waterways still goes on with only sporadic efforts to enforce better methods of dealing with this troublesome problem. It has been estimated that the operation of an adequate system of plants for the safe disposal of sewage and waste products will cost American cities $100,000,000 a year.[20] This is a heavy price to pay for the recreational use of our waterways but undoubtedly the trend is in this direction.

In the meantime the growing interest in water sports has led to the construction of outdoor swimming pools which are proving to be a very popular substitute for bathing beaches. Such pools, many of which are large and attractively de-

[19] Year Books of the National Recreation Association.
[20] Statement by H. B. Ward, National Director of Izaak Walton League, in *Proceedings* of the National Conference on Outdoor Recreation, Senate Document No. 117, 69th Congress, 1st Session, 1926, pp. 115–117.

signed, have become an important part of the equipment of many parks and playgrounds. In 1930 the number of public swimming pools reported in the year book of the National Recreation Association was 985, an increase of 80 per cent since 1923. The American Association of Pools and Beaches estimates that there are more than 3,500 swimming pools, both public and private, in the United States. Since swimming pools occupy comparatively small space and can be located in places where they are easily accessible to large numbers of people, they are not merely useful in cities that lack natural waterways, but supplement in an admirable manner even a well developed system of municipal beaches.

The extraordinary growth of bathing beaches and swimming pools has been accompanied by a similar increase in the use of water craft for pleasure purposes. While canoeing and sailing still have many enthusiastic devotees, the present widespread popularity of boating has come about through the recent development of the motor boat and especially of the small outboard and inboard types which have brought the sport within reach of people of moderate means. The number of registered motor boats under 16 gross tons, at least 75 per cent of which are used for pleasure purposes, increased from 130,826 in 1920 to 248,448 in 1930 (Table 16). These figures by no means include all the

TABLE 16.—NUMBER OF YACHTS AND MOTOR BOATS, BY CLASSES, 1900–1930

| Year | Documented yachts 16 gross tons and over[a] | | | | | Registered motor boats under 16 gross tons[b] |
	Steam	Motor	Sailing	House boats	Total documented yachts	
1900.............	423	58	971	5	1,457	
1905.............	487	467	1,058	6	2,018	
1910.............	392	690	301	19	1,402	
1915.............	308	1,024	206	18	1,556	
1920.............	176	1,181	144	17	1,518	130,826
1925.............	111	1,738	89	23	1,961	198,636
1930.............	74	3,132	85	24	3,315	248,448

[a] U. S. Bureau of Navigation, *Merchant Marine Statistics*, 1930, pp. 49–50.
[b] Compiled from list furnished by the U. S. Bureau of Navigation.

motor boats of small size, for a very considerable number fail to register in compliance with the law and those under 16 feet in length are not required to register. It is estimated that all types of motor boats in the United States, from the smallest outboards to the most palatial yachts, numbered in 1931 approximately 1,500,000.[21] This advance in motor boating has not been accompanied by a corresponding increase in older types of water craft. According to the Census of Manufactures, there was a marked decline in the number of sailboats, rowboats, and canoes constructed in this country between 1925 and 1929 (Table 17). This change in the type of water craft used for pleasure purposes is of great significance, for it is another important factor in the mounting costs of recreation.

TABLE 17.—NUMBER AND VALUE OF BOATS UNDER 5 GROSS TONS BUILT IN THE UNITED STATES, 1921–1929[a]

Year	Motor boats		Sail boats		Row boats		Canoes	
	Number	Value	Number	Value	Number	Value	Number	Value
1921....	808	$ 1,461,538						
1923....	939	2,713,772						
1925....	1,369	4,282,077	743	$426,901	10,940	$ 816,774	6,568	$477,906
1927....	2,466	6,272,631	799	513,456	12,868	1,074,127	5,960	453,453
1929....	14,194	11,207,350	699	499,461	6,795	434,657	4,736	344,536

[a] *United States Census of Manufactures*, 1925, 1927, 1929.

So rapidly have pleasure boats increased in number that docking and mooring accommodations have become entirely inadequate. There are thousands of small boat owners who hold no membership in yacht clubs and cannot afford to pay high fees for the use of privately maintained boat slips. One solution of this problem has been the construction and maintenance of harbors for pleasure craft by municipal park authorities who charge a reasonable rental for their use by boat owners. Chicago, Detroit, and San Francisco are among the cities that have utilized their park facilities for

[21] F. G. Menke, *All Sports Record Book* (1932 edition), p. 250.

the encouragement of boating among their citizens. The tendency is now in the direction of maintenance of municipal harbors for pleasure boats and as these harbor facilities increase boating no doubt will attract many more followers.

The popularity of boating is still further shown by the increase in yacht clubs, now numbering approximately 450, many of which maintain fine club houses and provide harbor facilities for various kinds of water craft from small sailing vessels to palatial motor yachts.[22] Week-end boat trips and longer vacation outings in small motor cruisers are common diversions of yacht club members. The new developments in motor boat construction make possible compact yet comfortable family cruisers, small in size, well adapted for short vacation trips. Outings of this kind are still limited to those possessing considerable means but are no longer thought of as pleasures attainable only by the wealthy.

Boat racing, which has long been a favorite diversion, has been given new impetus by the recent improvements in motor boats. In 1931 there were 130 sanctioned regattas sponsored by the American Power Boat Association and more than 4,000 other regattas were held in this country under the rules of that organization. Sailing races still remain popular and during 1931 more than 1,000 yachts were entered in the national regattas held under the auspices of the International Star Class Yacht Racing Association.[23] The American Canoe Association stages each year paddling and sailing canoe races which still attract considerable attention in spite of the rise of the speedier motor boats. The annual rowing races between college crews have for more than a half century been important events in the world of outdoor sport. The Poughkeepsie regatta, participated in by nine college crews in 1930, is witnessed each year by large crowds and is given wide publicity.

According to figures given out by the United States Bureau of Navigation, the registration of motor boats has continued to increase during 1930 and 1931 in spite of the

---

[22] Article on "Yachting," *Encyclopaedia Britannica*, 14th Edition, Vol. 23: 869.
[23] F. G. Menke, *All Sports Record Book* (1932 edition), p. 357.

financial depression. New York City is the leading motor boat harbor with Tampa, Philadelphia, Baltimore, and Norfolk ranking next in number of motor boat registrations. While the great boating centers are found in the cities along the seaboard and the Great Lakes, the recent improvement of small inland lakes and rivers has brought about a great expansion of boating in many sections of the country. Further extension of water sports is being made possible by the construction of artificial lakes and reservoirs for hydroelectric power plants. In those sections of the country where there are few natural lakes and rivers, these new water resources have great recreational value and efforts are being made to develop public parks along their shores. The development of the waterways of the nation for recreational purposes has as yet made only small beginnings and gives promise of becoming one of the most important movements in outdoor recreation.

Flying as a Sport.—While recent developments in aviation have been chiefly along commercial lines with chief emphasis upon rapid travel between distant places, the recreational aspects of flying have long been of considerable importance. More than a generation ago balloon ascensions and sensational parachute leaps constituted one of the popular attractions at county and state fairs. For years the public followed with great interest the outcome of so-called balloon races in which the prize was won by the pilot who could cover the longest distance before being forced to descend to the earth. As soon as airplanes had developed to the point where sustained flight for a considerable distance became possible, exhibition flights and air races became popular forms of entertainment in all sections of the country. In 1910 a ten-day aviation meet was held near Boston and was attended by as many as 75,000 people in one day.[24] The following year it was reported that a million dollars had been won in prizes by daring airplane pilots who risked their lives in races and

[24] Henry Woodhouse, "The Harvard-Boston Aviation Meet," *Independent*, 69: 676 (1910).

stunt flying for the amusement of spectators. Flying schools were established, aeronautical clubs were organized, gliding became an accepted sport in a few of the larger universities, and even school boys turned their attention to the building and flying of small model airplanes.

As airplanes have become more numerous, public interest in stunt flying has declined. Today the airplane plays its largest role as an amusement device in carrying aerial sightseers on short trips. Of the three and one-half million persons who flew during 1929, the vast majority went aloft because of the novelty of flying or to enjoy a brief sight seeing tour. With the continued development of larger airships with more comfortable accommodations for passengers on long trips, vacation tours by air are gaining in popularity. Already it is becoming more common to use airplanes for weekend pleasure trips and for rapid and convenient transportation to hunting and fishing grounds. A small but growing number of people have learned the art of flying so that they can operate their own airplanes as a means of recreation. If future improvements of airplanes make them easier to operate and reduce the cost of flying, they will undoubtedly become more widely used for recreational purposes.

Automobile Touring.—The close relation between the automobile and the recent interest in outdoor life can hardly be overestimated. With the development of this new type of rapid transportation adapted to the use of individual families, barriers of distance have been broken down in an unprecedented manner. Whereas formerly the leisure hours at the close of the working day had to be spent either at home or at adjacent places along routes of street car travel, the automobile makes possible the enjoyment of recreational facilities that would have been considered inaccessible in the days before motor cars were in common use. Parks for picnics and outings need no longer to be located along lines of rail transportation. The limits of the recreational community have been greatly extended with the result that people have a much wider range of choice as to methods of spending their leisure time. Of equal importance is the increase in the scope of leisure-time activities that can be carried on in a limited space of time. Through the aid of this rapid and convenient form of transportation a few hours of leisure can be utilized for a game of golf or tennis, or the family can enjoy a picnic in an outlying park, or a visit made to a bathing beach or some other place of recreation. This custom of seeking pleasure farther afield is one of the marked tendencies of the present day and has brought about a scattering of the people in their recreational life which has adversely affected local neighborhood organizations.

The growing tendency to travel in the search for recreation appears in its most striking form in the recent development of motor touring. During weekends and summer vacation periods the rural highways of the nation are crowded with automobile tourists on their way to places of scenic interest or perhaps with no definite goal in view except the pleasure of travel itself. The expanding network of improved highways penetrating even into the most remote places has opened up to the motor tourist vast regions with their lure of the strange and the unfamiliar. In 1931 nearly 900,000 private automobiles entered our national parks.[25] The Forest Service estimates that approximately 29,500,000 people travelled by automobile to the national forests during 1930. More than a million and a quarter United States automobiles crossed the Canadian border on 2 to 30 day permits for touring purposes during the year 1930.[26] Assuming that there were on the average 3.3 persons per car, more than 4,000,000 people motored into Canada that year, the majority of whom were presumably pleasure-seeking tourists. According to estimates prepared by the American Automobile Association, approximately 40,000,000 people enjoy vacation motor tours in this country each year.

This vast stream of tourist travel varies with the seasons and is greatest in those sections of the country that offer

[25] *Annual Report*, of the National Park Service, 1931.
[26] *Canada's Tourist Trade in 1930*, mimeographed report issued by the Department of Trade and Commerce, Dominion Bureau of Statistics, Canada.

the most popular vacation opportunities. Formerly it was almost entirely a summer movement, when the climate and the condition of the roads were most favorable for long trips. More recently winter vacations have become more common and the long lines of motor caravans head toward the south and southwest as cold weather approaches in the northern states. So great is this volume of long distance motor travel that special roadside accommodations have been built along the main routes of highway travel. The great vacation regions are becoming dotted with cottages and resorts of all descriptions and remote sections are being populated by permanent residents who find lucrative employment in catering to the needs of the motor tourists. Each year tourist resorts are being made more attractive by the building of golf courses, tennis courts, and other recreational features. A few years ago it was thought that this remarkable stream of tourist travel was a popular fad that would decline when the novelty of motoring had worn off. It is now apparent that automobile touring has gained its wide vogue because it is a convenient and comparatively inexpensive means of covering long distances in the search for new scenes where outdoor life may be enjoyed. The automobile provides for urban residents their most available means of escape from congested city districts and routine tasks. It is the lure of the out-of-doors and the open road that attracts them and until better means of transportation have been developed, motor touring will likely tend to increase among those who are able to afford this luxury.[27]

[27] For a fuller discussion of pleasure travel see the monograph in this series on *Communication Agencies and Social Life.*

CHAPTER IV

THE RISING TIDE OF SPORTS AND GAMES

THE first marked development of interest in athletic sports and games occurred in this country in the decades immediately following the Civil War. Prior to that time the emphasis was upon gymnastics and calisthenics which were designed to provide the physical training and exercise essential for the preservation of health. It was not until the seventies and eighties of last century that outdoor sports and games became sufficiently widespread to attract much public attention. Intercollegiate athletics and professional baseball gained their first real momentum during this period and proved to be the forerunners of the wide range of competitive athletic games that now enjoy such wide popularity.

The last decade, 1920–1930, appears now to mark the beginning of a second expansion of interest in outdoor games and athletic contests. Whereas the earlier period, to which reference has just been made, may be characterized as a pioneer recreational era when athletics was brought within reach of the few, this second period stands out because of its emphasis upon athletics for the many. The increasing amount of leisure, higher standards of living for large numbers of people, the breakdown of traditions against Sunday recreation, the growing belief that strenuous sports were a means to health, and the emphasis upon wholesome outdoor games in the war camp communities during the period of the World War, were among the factors that led to the development of an extraordinary demand for more ample facilities for athletic sports. So insistent has been this demand that large areas of our public parks have been turned into athletic fields and golf courses. For the first time in our history the crowds watching professional games are matched by the large numbers of people thronging the golf courses, tennis courts, and playfields. To a greater extent than ever before Americans are becoming a nation of players who get their thrill not merely by standing on the sidelines but by active participation in games of their choice.

Amateur Baseball.—Baseball, which has long been known as America's national game, has during the past decade found it increasingly difficult to maintain its former position as our most popular sport. From the point of view of the onlooker, football has for many proved to be a more attractive spectacle and golf makes a much stronger appeal to mature adults who wish to participate in outdoor games. Nevertheless, in spite of the increasing competition with other games, baseball still has a large and enthusiastic following. The 1930 Year Book of the National Recreation Association reported 241,766 players in the amateur baseball leagues sponsored by the departments of recreation in the cities from which figures were secured. Further evidence of the continued interest in amateur baseball is the success of the nation-wide junior baseball program sponsored by the American Legion. In their local, state, regional, and national tournaments held during the season of 1930 more than 300,000 boys participated.[1] The intramural baseball teams in the Chicago high schools increased in number two and one-half times during the past five years. The Brooklyn Department of Parks reported in 1927 that although 44 baseball diamonds were available, they were able to accommodate only one-third of the teams desiring to use them. The San Francisco Playground Commission reports that the interest in baseball is so great that it has been found impossible adequately to take care of all the young men wishing to play on the 11 regulation diamonds maintained by the Playground Department. The organized municipal baseball leagues of Houston, Texas, have 112 teams with 1,792 players. Louisville, Kentucky, reports 69 teams playing under the auspices

[1] *The American Legion Junior Handbook* (1931 Edition), p. 2.

of the Amateur Baseball Federation League. In addition, 78 teams of boys participated in the American Legion Junior Baseball Tournament in 1930. College baseball, which no longer attracts many spectators, is being played as usual and apparently has as many players as in the past. In the study of college athletics by the Carnegie Corporation published in 1929 it was found that in 50 institutions 10,215 students or 10 per cent of the total enrollment played intercollegiate or intramural baseball. On the basis of the proportion of the student body participating in the game, baseball stood fourth among college athletic sports, being outranked only by basketball, football, and tennis.[2]

In 1929, the total value of baseball goods manufactured amounted to $6,699,087. Since this is the first time that the Bureau of the Census reported baseball goods separately, no comparison can be made with other years. From the separate items listed under the heading of baseball goods we can get some indication of the widespread popularity of the game. During 1929 more than 8,500,000 balls (including playground balls) were manufactured; also 1,820,000 bats, 35,000 masks, and 900,000 mitts and gloves (Table 18). By far the larger part of this equipment is

TABLE 18.—QUANTITY AND VALUE OF SELECTED LIST OF SPORTING AND ATHLETIC GOODS, 1929[a]

Class	Quantity	Value (at factory)
Golf balls	33,832,800	$7,460,200
Golf clubs	3,166,380	9,722,610
Baseballs	8,514,624	3,261,411
Baseball bats	1,819,697	1,050,638
Baseball masks	35,690	110,847
Baseball mitts and gloves	932,157	1,820,035
Footballs	530,631	1,410,781
Basket balls and other inflated balls	1,382,460	1,641,224
Tennis balls	10,197,072	1,797,992
Tennis rackets	628,086	1,599,259
Boxing gloves (sets of 4)	60,979	440,730
Roller skates (pairs)	2,614,944	2,925,034
Ice skates (pairs)	684,964	1,782,172

[a] Compiled from *United States Census of Manufacturers*, 1929.

[2] H. J. Savage, *American College Athletics*, Carnegie Foundation Bulletin No. 23, pp. 114, 347.

purchased by amateur players. When the different classes of sporting goods are ranked according to the value of their annual output, baseball goods stand third, being outranked by golf goods and fishing apparatus.[3]

Baseball as played by amateurs has in recent years been profoundly affected by the growing popularity of playground ball. Originally developed as an adaptation of baseball for indoor use, this new game, which uses a large, soft ball, has increased rapidly in public favor because it requires comparatively little space, a minimum of equipment, and no great amount of training and practice in order to play sufficiently well to give enjoyment to both players and spectators. It is now so widely played throughout the country that it may be regarded as a well established modification of baseball made necessary by the increasing congestion of urban centers. In 1924, 161 cities reported 74,249 players of playground ball and in 1930 the cities reporting on this game had increased to 344 with 213,324 players.[4] It is quite clear from this evidence as well as from reports of municipal park systems that this new type of ball game has made great inroads upon regular baseball and gives some justification for the prediction that it may eventually become the game sponsored by amateurs while the game with the hard ball will be left largely in the hands of the professionals.

Tennis.—Tennis was introduced into this country about 1875 and for many years attracted very few players outside the membership of the more exclusive clubs. In 1881 the United States Lawn Tennis Association was organized with 33 member clubs, and under its direction the equipment and rules were standardized and tournaments were arranged for in different sections of the country. The first tournament to decide the national championships was held in 1881 and nine years later interest in tennis was still further stimulated by the establishment of the international Davis cup matches to determine the world championship.

[3] *United States Census of Manufactures,* 1929.
[4] Year Books of the National Recreation Association.

While tennis has attracted a wide following during recent years, complete figures showing the expansion of playing facilities and the increase in the number of players are not available. One indication of the increased vogue of the game is the growing number of member clubs of the United States Lawn Tennis Association. In 1910 these clubs numbered 160; in 1920 there were 294; and in 1930 they had increased to approximately 800. It is estimated that in 1930 these clubs had a total membership of between fifty and sixty thousand players who had available for their use about 5,500 courts. This by no means exhausts the privately maintained tennis facilities for there are many country clubs chiefly interested in golf that provide one or more courts for their members. In *Golfdom's* annual survey of golf courses in 1930 it was estimated that more than one-third of the golf clubs had built tennis courts numbering approximately 6,000.[5] This is largely a recent development and is another important indication of the growing popularity of tennis.

Of even greater significance from the point of view of the popularization of the game is the inclusion of tennis among the games sponsored by municipal park and recreational systems throughout the country. During the opening decade of the present century tennis courts began to be built by the park systems of some of the large cities, thereby starting a movement which has spread widely and made possible the development of tennis as a popular sport among the rank and file of the people. As early as 1905 the South Park System of Chicago had 100 public tennis courts. Ten years later they had more than trebled and were used during the playing season by 350,000 people. In 1930 there were nearly 750 public tennis courts in Chicago, outnumbering by at least 200 the courts maintained in that city by private clubs.

In 1924, when the National Recreation Association included for the first time in its Year Book information concerning public tennis courts, 410 cities reported 4,865

---

[5] *The Golf Market* (1930 edition).

courts. Eight years later in 1931 the number of courts as reported by 621 cities had increased to 8,804, an increase of 81 per cent during this period. The spread of the movement is also shown by the fact that there were 211 more cities reporting courts in 1931 than in 1924, a gain of 51 per cent. This movement to provide public tennis courts has made its greatest progress in large cities and the least advance in cities of small size. In 1930, 87 per cent of the cities over 50,000 population had made some provision for public tennis courts while only 5.6 per cent of the cities between 2,500 and 10,000 population reported that they furnished playing facilities for this game. In the cities where public tennis courts are provided there is on the average one court for each 5,000 people. There are, however, 2,623 cities above 2,500 population which did not report public tennis courts in 1930. The widespread use of the public courts is readily apparent to every observer. According to an estimate made by the Public Parks Committee of the United States Lawn Tennis Association, there were in 1930 more than 1,200,000 public park tennis players.[6] Since 1923 the park players have been holding an annual tournament to determine the public parks championship. In 1930 fifty-four players representing 30 cities competed in this tournament.

Further evidence concerning the increasing popularity of tennis is furnished by the growing interest in tennis among college students. Thirty years ago tennis was played seriously in comparatively few of the higher educational institutions and only a small number of courts were available. At the present time nearly every college and university has its tennis team which competes in intercollegiate tournaments. As a voluntary intramural sport, tennis has gained wide vogue among college students and usually has as many participants during the playing season as the facilities permit. Tennis courts are now found on practically every campus although few institutions have a sufficient number to meet the demand. Ten of the largest private universities

---

[6] Mimeographed report issued December 8, 1930.

have a total of 315 courts, an average of 31 for each institution. The number of courts at state universities, based
on information from 28 institutions of this class, range
from 4 to 60 with an average of 20 at each university. One
hundred and fifty colleges and universities, widely representative of all types of collegiate institutions, provide
1,775 tennis courts for their students, the median number
for each institution being 8.[7] On the basis of this sample it
seems safe to estimate that there are between four and five
thousand courts at the institutions of college grade in this
country.

When one adds to the tennis playing facilities that have
already been mentioned, the courts provided by high
schools and private secondary schools, those furnished by
industrial concerns for their employees, those attached to
summer camps, those maintained by hotels at summer and
winter resorts for their guests, those belonging to private
homes, and those operated on a commercial basis as pay
courts, it is apparent that the opportunities for playing
this game are widespread and reach many different classes
and groups of people. While an accurate statement of the
total number of tennis courts in this country is impossible,
a conservative estimate would be 25,000, more than half
of which have been constructed during the past fifteen
years.

The increasing production of tennis goods tends to
corroborate the above evidence concerning the rapid
growth of tennis as a popular outdoor sport. The total
value of tennis goods produced by American manufacturers
in 1927, the first year that tennis goods were listed separately in the Census report, amounted to $3,227,552. In
1929 the manufactured value of such goods was $4,650,543,
an increase during this two-year period of 44.1 per cent.
This rate of increase was considerably less than that for
golf goods but was greater than the rate for sporting and

[7] Compiled from data furnished by the various institutions. Figures showing
the number of tennis courts at 39 colleges and universities were published b
American Lawn Tennis in its issues of April 20 and July 20, 1930.

athletic goods as a whole. Some idea of the widespread vogue of tennis can be gained from the fact that more than 10,000,000 tennis balls were manufactured in this country in 1929.[8]

As a result of the recent expansion of tennis playing facilities and the increasing number of players, tennis is rapidly losing its former provincial character and is tending to become a national game in all parts of the country. Traditionally, tennis has belonged to the large cities of the North Atlantic seaboard where the game was first introduced about fifty-five years ago. For many years this section has remained the leading tennis center of the United States. New York has been the headquarters of the United States Lawn Tennis Association and 40 per cent of the member clubs of this organization are located in the New England and the Middle Atlantic states. The most important national tournaments have been held at clubs in or near New York, Philadelphia, Providence, and Boston. For many years the best players were largely an eastern product. From 1900 to 1920 the winners of the national intercollegiate singles were students of Harvard, Yale, Princeton, Pennsylvania, and Columbia. Twenty-nine or more than three-fourths of the 37 men ranked among the first ten players between 1900 and 1910 had their homes along the North Atlantic seaboard.[9]

While the Northeast still retains a large share of its former leadership in tennis, its position has become less secure as the game has taken root in other sections of the country. At the present time there is a fairly equitable distribution of both public and private playing facilities in all the geographical divisions (Table 19). The United States Lawn Tennis Association has organized 13 sectional associations which cover the entire country. While the

---

[8] *United States Census of Manufactures,* 1927, 1929. Tennis goods valued at $129,763 were imported into this country in 1929. The value of tennis goods exported that year cannot be determined since this item is not reported separately. See *Foreign Commerce and Navigation of the United States,* 1929, Vol. 1, pp. 204, 555.

[9] Compiled from information furnished by the secretary of the United States Lawn Tennis Association.

East is still the stronghold of the private clubs, the Middle West has forged ahead with its public courts and the Far West is building up a new tennis center on the Pacific Coast. The gradual shift of tennis leadership that has been taking place in recent years is shown by the fact that since 1920 eastern institutions have won the national inter-

TABLE 19.—NUMBER OF PUBLIC TENNIS COURTS, BY GEOGRAPHICAL DIVISIONS, 1930[a]

Geographical division	Number of public tennis courts	Number per 100,000 urban population	Geographical division	Number of public tennis courts	Number per 100,000 urban population
United States........	8,085	12	New England.........	682	10
			South Atlantic........	674	12
East North Central...	2,536	15	West South Central....	377	9
Middle Atlantic.......	1,870	9	East South Central....	248	9
Pacific..............	812	15	Mountain............	173	12
West North Central...	713	13			

[a] Compiled from the 1930 Year Book of the National Recreation Association.

collegiate singles but twice. The South, Southwest, Middle West, and Far West furnished more than one-half of the first ten ranking American players between 1920 and 1930, whereas less than one-fourth had come from these sections during the first decade of this century. The country no longer looks to eastern players alone for contenders in the Davis cup matches. Players from all sections of the country participate in the important tournaments and 15 states were represented among the 37 ranking players for the year 1930.

The growth of tennis is especially significant because its appeal is to participants rather than to spectators. Rarely are large crowds of people found at tournaments and those that do attend are likely to be persons who play the game themselves and are as much interested in the skill displayed as in the outcome of the matches. The recent efforts to build up public support for professional tennis have not been very successful. Tennis brings its chief pleasure to those who play and its wide popularity is at least partly due to the fact that the game can be enjoyed by those who possess only a moderate amount of skill. So great has been the demand for tennis playing facilities that the playing season is being extended through the construction of all-weather courts. In some places also the daily hours of play have been lengthened through the device of night illumination. Since tennis does not require a large amount of space and can be played with comparatively inexpensive equipment, it is likely to remain a popular form of outdoor recreation among those vigorous enough to enjoy a fairly strenuous sport.

Golf.—The spectacular growth of golf during recent years is unparalleled in the history of American outdoor sports. Prior to the World War golf had attained considerable popularity especially in the large cities, and approximately 800 golf courses had been constructed. It was, however, quite generally regarded as a game best suited for those who had a considerable amount of leisure and had sufficient financial resources to hold membership in a private country club. The new enthusiasm for outdoor recreation for adults as well as children which developed during and immediately following the war greatly stimulated public interest in golf and strengthened the demand for more playing facilities. Between 1916 and 1923 golf courses in the United States grew from 742 to 1,903, an increase of 156.5 per cent. This extraordinary expansion of golf courses was not merely maintained but surpassed during the succeeding seven-year period, for in 1930 they numbered 5,856, a gain of 207.7 per cent (Table 20).

While the vast majority of these courses are private, a rapidly growing number are municipally-owned and open to the general public, usually upon the payment of a small fee. In 1910 there were in operation 24 public golf courses, almost all of which were located in large cities in the northern and eastern part of the country. Between 1910 and 1920 these public courses slightly more than trebled, and in 1931 according to figures issued by *Golfdom*, there were 543 courses maintained by cities and towns in 46 states.[10] In spite of this great increase in municipal golf courses, this form of public recreation is found in less than one-fifth of American cities. So popular are these public courses that it is not infrequent for them to have a continuous stream of players from dawn to dusk during the weekends of the summer months. The great demand of the public for more golf playing facilities has led to the development, especially in the large metropolitan centers, of daily fee

TABLE 20.—NUMBER OF GOLF COURSES, BY GEOGRAPHICAL DIVISIONS, 1916, 1923, 1930[a]

Geographical division	Number of courses			Per cent increase, 1923–1930
	1916	1923	1930	
United States..........................	742	1,903	5,856	207.7
New England.........................	182	252	495	96.4
Middle Atlantic......................	205	398	914	129.6
East North Central...........	124	403	1,318	227.0
West North Central..................	53	292	1,018	248.6
South Atlantic.......................	80	199	614	208.5
East South Central..................	22	76	230	202.6
West South Central..................	27	87	550	530.0
Mountain............................	12	69	214	210.1
Pacific.........	37	127	503	295.4

[a] Compiled from *The Golf Market* (1929 and 1930 editions), published by *Golfdom*, Chicago. These figures, taken from *Golfdom's* annual survey of golf courses, are considerably larger than those given by other authorities. Fraser's *International Golf Year Book* for 1930 lists 4,669 golf courses, while the *Golfer's Year Book* gives a total of 4,262. These discrepancies are at least partially explained by the difficulty of keeping pace with the rapidly increasing number of courses. *Golfdom's* interest in the business side of golf necessitates a comprehensive list of private and public courses and it is believed that this list is fairly accurate.

courses operated on a commercial basis. There were approximately 700 of these courses in 1931, the vast majority of which have been constructed since 1925.

Golf was first introduced along the North Atlantic seaboard and its most rapid advance for many years was confined to the northern and eastern states. In 1916, the New England, Middle Atlantic, and East North Central

[10] *The Golf Market* (1931 edition). *Municipal Golf Courses in the United States*, issued by the Public Links Section of the United States Golf Association, contains a list of 291 municipal courses operating in 1930 but it is stated that the list is not complete.

states had two-thirds of all the golf courses and were the only geographical divisions with more than 100 golf courses each. Between 1916 and 1930 golf made such rapid progress in the remaining divisions in the West and South that in 1930 they had 53 per cent of the total number of golf courses throughout the country (Table 20).

As would be expected, the largest number of golf courses are found in the states with the largest urban population. When, however, the states are ranked according to the number of golf courses per 100,000 urban population, the urban states make a poorer showing than do many of the rural states. New York, for example, which ranks first in number of golf courses, had, in 1930, 5 courses per 100,000 urban population, and Illinois, which ranks second, had 7 courses per 100,000, while Iowa had 21 and Kansas 30 per 100,000 urban population. Even such a golf center as the metropolitan district of Chicago, which in 1930 boasted 273 golf courses, had barely 7 courses per 100,000 people.

TABLE 21.—NUMBER OF GOLF COURSES AND THE URBAN POPULATION PER COURSE, BY GEOGRAPHICAL DIVISIONS, 1930[a]

Geographical division	Number of golf courses	Urban population per course	Geographical division	Number of golf courses	Urban population per course
United States.........	5,856	11,775	West South Central....	550	8,049
			Pacific...............	503	11,003
East North Central...	1,318	12,742	New England.........	495	12,751
West North Central...	1,018	5,457	East South Central....	230	12,081
Middle Atlantic.......	914	22,323	Mountain............	214	6,812
South Atlantic........	614	9,280			

[a] Compiled from *The Golf Market* (1930 edition).

In spite of the growth of this game in the industrial area of the North and East, the golf playing facilities have not kept pace with the expansion of cities. In general the western and southern portions of the United States seem better provided with golf courses than the more urbanized sections when judged by the number of urban people for each course (Table 21).

The center of municipal golf course development is located in the East North Central states, which have a much higher proportion of the total number of the municipal courses than they have of the total number of all golf courses. In New England municipal golf course construction has gone forward very slowly, while the South and Far West have made more consistent progress in this direction. Public golf courses were first provided in large cities and it is only recently that this movement has made much headway in the smaller municipalities. In 1923 two-thirds of the public golf courses were maintained by cities with a population of 100,000 or more; in 1930 the cities of this population class had only half of the total number of such courses.[11] A considerable number of municipal courses have been constructed during 1930 and 1931 in connection with unemployment relief operations. Because of the financial stringency golf course construction was limited almost entirely during 1931 to public and daily fee courses.[12]

This extraordinary expansion of golf courses, both public and private, is bringing the game within reach of increasing numbers of people. The total number of golf players in the United States is not known but estimates vary from two to three million. *Golfdom's* estimate of more than two million players is based on the assumption that the average number of players at private clubs is 275 and at municipal and daily fee courses 725.[13] The total membership of the 3,961 private golf clubs listed in the 1931 edition of *The Golfer's Year Book*, based upon membership reports of 53 per cent of the clubs, may be estimated to be approximately 880,000. If we add to this number 200,000 to include players who belong to the families of club members, we have a total of more than a million players in slightly less than 4,000 private clubs. The chairman of the Public Links Section of the United States Golf Association estimates that more

[11] Compiled from data given in *Municipal Golf Courses in the United States*, issued by the Public Links Section of the United States Golf Association, New York, 1931.
[12] *The Golf Market* (1931 edition).
[13] *The Golf Market* (1931–1932 edition).

than 500,000 players use the municipal golf courses.[14] The patrons of the 700 daily fee courses must number between 350,000 and 400,000 each year. While all the above figures are estimates, they seem to be sufficiently conservative to warrant the conclusion that at least two million people in this country have taken up golf as one of their leisure-time activities. During the past ten years the number of players has more than trebled and the game is still on a rising tide of popularity. Reports from 291 public golf courses showed a total of nine hole rounds in excess of eighteen million during 1930.[15] *Golfdom's* estimate of the number of rounds played in 1931 is 68,796,000 for the 18 hole courses and 24,723,400 for the nine hole courses, a total of 93,519,400 rounds played on all types of golf courses throughout the country that year.

When consideration is given to the financial aspects of golf, it is apparent that it has developed into a huge enterprise involving many millions of dollars for its annual maintenance. According to the Census of Manufactures, the value of golf equipment manufactured in 1929 amounted to $21,067,216, which is 37.4 per cent of the total value of sporting and athletic goods manufactured that year. The cost to the consumer is of course far in excess of this factory value, for his purchases are made at retail prices. No other single sport approaches golf in the amount of money annually invested in equipment. Moreover, the manufacture of golf goods is on the upward trend as is shown by the gain of 71.8 per cent in the value of such goods during the two-year period, 1927–1929.

However great may be the amount spent for golf equipment, this expenditure represents only a small fraction of the total expense of golf. Because of golf's extravagant use of space, the golf courses in the United States require approximately 500,000 acres of land, the vast majority of which is located either within or adjacent to cities where the land values are high. *Golfdom's* statement that $830,-

[14] *The Golfer's Year Book* (1931 edition), p. 655.

[15] *Municipal Golf Courses in the United States,* issued by the Public Links Section of the United States Golf Association, New York, 1931.

039,298 is the value of the golf plants throughout the country may be accepted as a conservative figure, considerably less than the billion dollar estimate that is frequently made.[16] Many of the golf clubs maintain expensive club houses and the total amount spent by the members of private clubs mounts to a very high figure. On the assumption that members of 18 hole private clubs spend on an average for dues and other club expenses $500 a year, and that members of 9 hole private clubs spend $250 annually, the total yearly expenditures of members of these clubs amount to approximately $450,000,000. To this should be added the more modest expenditures of the patrons of the municipal and daily fee courses who manage to play the game at an annual cost of perhaps $50 to $100 per capita. Since these figures do not include the money spent on golf tournaments, the cost of golf lessons, the expense involved in travel to and from golf courses, and other miscellaneous expenses such as golf clothing, it would seem that the annual cost of golf to the American people must be considerably more than half a billion dollars.

One of the striking things about this popularity of golf is the rapidity with which the game has swept over the country. As recently as 1916 there were 4 states with no golf courses, 16 states with less than 5 each, 28 states each of which had fewer than 10 courses, and only one state with as many as one hundred. Fourteen years later in 1930 there was only one state with less than 10 courses, and there were 18 states with courses ranging from 100 to 400 in number.[17] Enthusiastic followers of the game predict that this upward trend will continue until at least 20,000 golf courses are available for use. One of the difficulties in the way of this further expansion, especially in the large cities, is the increasing scarcity of conveniently located land that can be purchased without excessive cost. A game that makes such heavy demands upon space that it can accommodate no more than 2 players per acre at one time must neces-

[16] *The Golf Market* (1931 edition).
[17] *The Golf Market* (1929 and 1930 editions).

sarily be an expensive sport in urban districts and cannot readily be expanded to the point where it can be made available for a large portion of the people. There is much room, however, for the further expansion of golf in small cities and towns and it is significant that much of the recent advance made by this game has been in these smaller places where nine hole courses are being constructed and operated at a sufficiently low cost to be within the means of a small membership. The utilization of park lands for public golf courses has as yet made only a small beginning and will doubtless continue until this game becomes a part of the recreational program of the majority of municipalities. Since golf makes a strong appeal to the young and old of both sexes and is of such a nature that it can be enjoyed by those who possess only moderate skill and yet is so difficult that it can never be entirely mastered, its further expansion is assured in spite of the fact that it requires a large outlay of capital for playing facilities as well as a considerable expenditure of both time and money on the part of individual players.

Winter Sports.—Outdoor winter sports dependent upon snow and ice are necessarily limited to the northern states and have made greatest headway in those cities where low temperatures are fairly continuous during the winter months. The modern playground movement, which had its origin in the large northern cities, was at first concerned with summer rather than winter sports. When year round recreational activities began to be emphasized, field houses and community centers were built in order to provide the space needed for indoor sports and games that seemed most suitable for the long winter season. Outdoor winter sports were left entirely to individual initiative and since they were dependent upon the weather and the local topography they attracted a considerable following only in the most favorably located places.

The striking change that has taken place in outdoor winter sports during the past two decades has come about largely through organized public efforts to provide more satisfactory facilities for their enjoyment. By flooding suitably located areas skating and hockey rinks are provided which are available for use when temperatures are too mild for safe skating on lakes and rivers. This not merely extends the skating season but also removes the element of danger and makes possible skating in communities where there are no conveniently located natural bodies of water. In a similar manner snow sports have been given wider vogue through the construction of toboggan chutes and slides, the closing of streets suitable for coasting, and the building of high trestles for ski jumps in places where natural inclines do not exist. The more progressive recreation departments in cities located in the snow belt organize programs of winter sports with meets and tournaments that attract thousands of participants and spectators. For the comfort and convenience of participants heated shelters are provided where refreshments can be secured, wraps checked, and equipment rented. Very few municipalities furnished facilities of this kind twenty years ago, and the progress that has been made in this direction is largely an accomplishment of the past decade.

The recent development of interest in skiing furnishes a good illustration of the growing popularity of outdoor winter sports. In 1904 the National Ski Association of America was organized in Michigan by a half dozen Norwegian ski clubs with a membership of about 150. This organization grew slowly and in 1920 consisted of only 25 clubs with a membership of eight or nine hundred. During the past decade the number of clubs increased to 110 with a membership in 1930 of approximately 7,000. The tournaments increased during this same period from 15 to 125 while the number of spectators grew from approximately 8,000 to 400,000.[18] The sport of skiing is of course by no means limited to the spectacular ski jumps in which the public is mainly interested. Ski tours or hikes over hill and mountain trails have in recent years become popular among

[18] From information furnished by Gustave E. Lindboe, formerly executive secretary of the American Ski Association.

ski enthusiasts and are greatly increasing the number of participants in this sport. Ski clubs maintain cabins and huts along trails in the White and Green Mountains in the East and in the Rockies, Cascades, and Sierra Nevada mountains in the West.

Ice skating apparently attracts more participants than does any other winter sport and it has recently been made more popular and widespread through the construction of artificial rinks in parks and playing fields. In St. Paul, Minnesota, during the winter of 1928 eighteen skating rinks were in use for a seven weeks season with a total attendance of 387,187 participants. Ten hockey rinks were used by 60 teams which played more than 200 games. More than a thousand skaters participated in skating meets with spectators numbering 46,000. The city of Minneapolis reports that the total attendance of skaters at public rinks is approximately one and a half million.[19] There has been sufficient interest in figure skating to organize the United States Figure Skating Association which has held annual championship meets since 1920. The amateur speed skaters have formed at least 12 skating associations which are banded together nationally in the Amateur Skating Union of the United States.

In 1924 several colleges and universities in the northeastern states and Canada organized the Intercollegiate Winter Sports Union which has been conducting meets for college students featuring ski jumps, cross country and down hill ski races, snowshoe races, and skating events. The Lake Placid Club in the Adirondacks has become the popular eastern center for winter sports and the meets held there in recent years have attracted many thousands of people. Perhaps the most important western center is Minneapolis, where there is held each year an elaborate winter sports program which includes figure skating pageants, ice carnivals, ice circuses, treasure hunts on skis and snowshoes, snow modeling contests, and ice yacht races.

[19] "Growth of Winter Sports," *The American City*, 39: 93–96 (1928).

Interest in winter sports has greatly increased the travel to those national parks that provide facilities for this form of recreation. Eleven of these parks are now operated on a year round schedule and those specializing in winter sports are Yosemite, Mount Rainier, Sequoia, General Grant, and Rocky Mountain. The National Park Service estimates that 100,000 visitors participated in winter sports in Yosemite during the winter of 1929–1930, a high record that was maintained during the following winter. Winter travel to General Grant Park more than doubled during the winter of 1930–1931 and the winter use of Mount Rainier Park has also greatly increased.[20]

This growing popularity of outdoor winter sports is especially significant since their appeal is primarily to participants rather than to spectators. Crowds get thrills out of spectacular ski jumps and championship ice races but cold weather discourages attendance at such contests. Outdoor winter recreation has made rapid progress because of the large numbers of people who desire to participate in vigorous sports during a season of the year when summer games are not available. Through the recent development of winter sports year round outdoor recreation has been made possible for hundreds of thousands of people who formerly enjoyed active games only during the summer season.

Trends in Athletic Sports.—The most notable change in the field of athletic sports is the growing popularity of games that appeal more to participants than to observers. Athletic sports are no longer merely spectacular events to be witnessed from the side lines. Recent years have seen an enormous expansion of playing facilities designed not primarily for trained professional athletes but for the general public. Evidence of this trend has been given in the preceding paragraphs which have pointed out the great advances in providing playing fields, tennis courts, golf courses, and facilities for winter sports. The public follows with great interest the records of the great golfers, whose

[20] Annual Reports of National Park Service, 1930, 1931.

names become widely known throughout the country, but their achievements are to be emulated rather than to be observed as a thrilling spectacle. The most enthusiastic supporters of athletic sports today are not the baseball or football fans but those who enjoy the thrill of active participation in the games they themselves play.

Another trend of real significance is the growing interest in outdoor sports of a less strenuous type suitable for mature people of both sexes and those unable to indulge in vigorous exercise. Golf is preeminently such a game which can be played by both young and old. Tennis, squash racquets, and handball make heavier demands upon strength but are far removed from the rougher athletic sports. Other examples of popular sports of the less strenuous sort are lawn bowling, quoits, horseshoes, roque, archery, fly casting, and volley ball, all of which are frequently a regular part of municipal recreation programs and are participated in by many thousands of people. It has been through the provision of facilities for sports of this kind that there has developed such widespread interest in playing rather than in watching games.

The increasing number of people who insist on participating in outdoor sports and games has created the problem not merely of providing the playing facilities but of securing the needed play space conveniently located for the use of urban residents. Some of the most popular outdoor games are extravagant in the use of space and therefore serious limitations are faced when attempts are made to bring them within reach of larger numbers of people. A golf course provides for no more than 2 people per acre at any one time. A baseball field can accomodate 9 players per acre. Tennis, which is more economical in the use of space, can crowd 7 courts on one acre which will provide playing facilities for 28 people. It is readily apparent that these games which enjoy such wide vogue cannot easily be made accessible to the mass of urban people as long as the present crowded conditions in cities continue to exist. The present municipal park acreage is far from sufficient for this purpose even if it were all turned into golf courses and play-fields. Public park lands are increasing in extent each year but problems of finance as well as of space prevent rapid progress in this direction. If the trend toward wider partic-ipation in outdoor sports continues, it will be necessary for large numbers of people to content themselves with such games as quoits, roque, horseshoes, and volley ball which require a minimum of space for their enjoyment. Perhaps the problem of space may lead to an adaptation of existing games or the invention of new ones designed to meet the limitations of the urban environment.

Closely associated with the increased interest in outdoor recreation is the daylight saving movement which during recent years has gained the greatest share of its support among urban residents desirous of an additional hour of daylight for outdoor sports at the close of the working day. The daylight saving plan, which involves setting the clock one hour ahead during the summer months, came in as a war measure in Europe in 1916 and was widely heralded as a device that made possible decreased expenditures for artificial illumination. A similar plan was advocated by chambers of commerce and other organizations in some of the large industrial centers in the eastern states without success until 1918 when Congress passed a daylight saving law as an emergency war measure. Daylight saving under the federal law was put in operation throughout the entire country during the summers of 1918 and 1919 and was then discontinued by the repeal of the law over President Wilson's veto.

Following the abolition of this daylight saving plan as a war measure, several states passed laws permitting cities and towns to adopt daylight saving when approved by a majority of their voters. This movement, which was led by the National Daylight Saving Association, made slow headway because of the widespread opposition of agricul-tural leaders and of some labor organizations. During the past ten years daylight saving has been adopted on a state-wide basis in two states, Massachusetts and Rhode Island,

and has gained some foothold in 15 other states.[21] Nearly all of these states are located in the industrial sections of the North and East; the movement has not spread to the South and has made few inroads west of the Mississippi River. While the extension of this movement is not rapid, the trend is decidedly in the direction of adjustménts that give longer evenings of daylight for outdoor games. In 1927 Ohio accomplished this purpose by adopting eastern standard time the year round. Practically all of the lower peninsula of Michigan has done likewise and North Dakota in 1929 changed from mountain to central standard time. The cities in New Hampshire effect daylight saving by beginning the working day one hour earlier instead of setting the clock forward. Between 1925 and 1930 the number of cities and towns in New York observing daylight saving increased from 130 to 190 and in New Jersey from 88 to 118.[22] On the other hand, daylight saving in Illinois and Indiana has not been extended beyond the metropolitan region of Chicago. In most of the states where daylight saving is permitted, it has been possible to keep the plan in operation only in the large cities. Taking the country as a whole, the growing demand for more time for outdoor sports at the close of the working day is being met through the device of outdoor illumination rather than through the daylight saving plan. Night illumination of tennis courts, ball fields, golf courses, and playgrounds has been making rapid progress in many of the cities throughout all sections of the country and is forcing into the background the less expensive plan of adjusting the hours of the working day so as to have more daylight for recreation.

[21] New York, New Jersey, Connecticut, Maine, Vermont, New Hampshire, Delaware, Illinois, Indiana, Ohio, Michigan, Minnesota, Wisconsin, North Dakota, and Pennsylvania. In three of these states—Connecticut, Maine, and Wisconsin—laws have been passed forbidding daylight saving but they are not strictly enforced.

[22] The Merchants' Association of New York is at present the leading advocate of daylight saving and collects and publishes each year the only available statistics on the subject.

CHAPTER V

SPORT AS A PUBLIC SPECTACLE

ALONG with the development of widespread recreational facilities that have brought opportunity for
active play to millions of people, there has been an unprecedented building of grandstands and stadia to accommodate the crowds who find their enjoyment in watching
competitive sports and games. This interest in sport as a
public spectacle is nothing new. The Olympic games in
early Greece and the gladiatorial combats of Rome were
events of great importance witnessed by thousands of
people. The lure of those early sports and physical contests
was as compelling as that of the modern prize fight or
football game and the response of the public was as eager
and unrestrained as is the case at the present time. The
new factors in the situation are the extraordinary crowds,
the multiplicity of games and sports that provide opportunity for spectators, the extensive publicity and advertising designed to increase public interest and support, and
the development of great business enterprises that make
millions of dollars out of the commercialization of sport.
It has been the exploitation of athletic sports for private
profit that has made so widespread this form of public
entertainment and has led to the fear voiced by many people
that Americans are turning into a nation of spectators.

Professional Baseball.—For fifty years the fortunes of
professional baseball teams have been eagerly followed by
enthusiastic supporters of the game. No other athletic
sport has had such a long and consistent record of attendance throughout the entire country. Recently college football has occupied the limelight and occasionally a prizefight
attracts enormous crowds, but baseball fans still remain
sufficiently numerous to give this game high rank among

[83]

business enterprises. More than ten million people attended the games of the two major baseball leagues during the season of 1930, approximately a million increase over 1920 Table 22). This increase, however, has not kept pace with

TABLE 22.—ATTENDANCE AT BASEBALL GAMES, 1920–1930ᵃ

Year	Two major leagues		Class AA minor leagues	
	Attendance (in thousands)	Index number (1923 = 100)	Attendance (in thousands)	Index number (1923 = 100)
1920...................	9,134	105.0		
1921...................	8,620	99.1		
1922...................	8,824	101.4		
1923...................	8,702	100.0	4,781	100
1924...................	9,605	110.4	5,303	111
1925...................	9,546	109.7	4,809	101
1926...................	9,837	113.0	5,122	107
1927...................	9,937	114.2	5,125	107
1928...................	9,121	104.8	5,352	112
1929...................	9,592	110.2	4,937	103
1930...................	10,185	117.0	4,616	96

ᵃ Compiled from information supplied by the presidents of the American League, the National League, the American Association, the International League, and the Pacific Coast League.

the growth of population in the eleven cities in which the major league teams play. While the population in these cities increased 20.5 per cent between 1920 and 1930, attendance at games increased only 11.5 per cent. Even though this increase is not great, it is significant that the curve of attendance continues to mount upward each year. Facilities for spectators have expanded during the past decade and at many games of winning teams seating space has been at a premium. On the other hand, it is becoming more difficult to secure public support of teams that fail to make a good showing. Unless the contest throughout the season is close with the final winners of the pennant always in doubt, public interest slackens.

For more than twenty-five years the playing season of the major leagues has closed with the "world series" of games in which the contenders are the teams that have won the pennant in their respective leagues. Since the games played in this series vary slightly in number from year to

[84]

year and moreover are played in cities of different size, a comparison of the annual attendance and receipts is not of great value in measuring the extent of public support. The differences, however, between the two past decades may be worth noting. The total attendance during the decade 1911–1920 was 1,730,900 and during the past decade, 2,455,203, an increase of 41 per cent. The total number of games played during each decade was exactly the same but since the world series ordinarily attracts capacity crowds, this increased attendance should perhaps be regarded simply as a measure of the increased accommodations for spectators. The fact that there was a 99 per cent increase in the total receipts for the last decade as over against the preceding decade (from $4,734,607 to $9,427,118) indicates the mounting cost of baseball if not a greater public interest in the championship series.[1]

In addition to the two major leagues which occupy the center of attention in professional baseball, there have been for many years various minor leagues now operating in approximately 140 cities widely scattered throughout the country. Since 1903 these minor leagues have been banded together into the National Association of Professional Baseball Leagues which in 1931 had a membership of 18 leagues divided into five classes largely upon the basis of the size of the cities supporting them. All the evidence that it was possible to secure indicates that the minor leagues are finding it increasingly difficult to operate on a profitable basis. The attendance records of the three leagues belonging to Class AA, the highest ranking division among the minors, show a decline of nearly three quarters of a million between 1928 and 1930. Four of the smaller leagues suspended operations during 1930; three others experienced a 21 per cent decline in attendance between 1927 and 1930.[2]

The slow increase in attendance at major league games and the declining support of the minor leagues in all sections of the country give some justification for the prediction

[1] F. G. Menke, *All Sports Record Book* (1931 edition), p. 57.
[2] Information furnished by the presidents of the various minor leagues.

that baseball is approaching the peak of its popularity as far as public interest in professional games is concerned. Baseball no doubt is as fascinating to watch as in the past but it faces much more competition than ever before. The vastly greater opportunities for participation in many different kinds of sports keep away from professional baseball games many who formerly were enthusiastic fans. The public parks and bathing beaches and golf courses are crowded on summer afternoons and weekends and this competition has been especially disastrous for baseball in the smaller cities where patrons of the game are relatively few. In an effort to increase attendance many of the minor league teams have adopted the plan of playing games at night in illuminated ball parks. While this experiment has not been uniformly successful, the technical difficulties have been largely overcome and this may ultimately prove to be the solution of their problem of financial support.

In spite of the apparent recent failure of baseball to compete successfully with other leisure-time attractions, there can be no doubt of its wide hold on the American people. An annual attendance at professional games of at least 20,000,000 places it in the first rank of American sports and it will take a much more serious decline than is at present evident for baseball to lose its position of preeminence. When we consider the additional millions who attend semi-professional and amateur games played in public parks and elsewhere, the large numbers who follow the games through the radio and the sport pages of the newspapers, and the crowds around the bulletin boards of newspaper offices watching the play-by-play report of the games, it is quite clear that baseball during six months of each year provides a very considerable share of the passive amusement of the nation.

College Football.—The American game of football is an adaptation of English Rugby and was developed by the colleges along the North Atlantic seaboard about 1870. It proved to be more popular than Association football, which had also been introduced into this country, but was subjected to much criticism because of its roughness. In 1884, upon recommendation of its committee on athletics, Harvard abolished football on the ground that it "is brutal, demoralizing to players and spectators, and extremely dangerous."[3] The game, however, continued to make headway among the eastern colleges and as early as the eighties and nineties of last century large and enthusiastic crowds were not uncommon at the more important games. An article on football published in 1887 stated that "the enormous crowd, the coaches filled with men and horns, the masses and shades of color among the spectators, the perpetual roar of cheers, including the peculiar slogans of almost all the eastern colleges, combine to make up a spectacle such as no other intercollegiate game can offer."[4] In 1905 new rules were adopted abolishing mass formations and providing for a more open style of play which proved to be more satisfactory to the spectators as well as less dangerous for the players. With the development of this new type of game, football greatly increased its popularity and since then has maintained its place as a leading American sport although limited in its playing season to a few months during the autumn of each year.

During the past few years, in spite of enormous crowds at many of the games, there has been considerable discussion concerning the future of college football and its possible decline in public favor. Keen observers have pointed out the fact that in certain sections students seem less excited than formerly about the outcome of the football season and that the general public quickly loses interest in teams that fall below championship caliber. In order to get facts that would show whether college football is on the wane, a questionnaire was sent out to more than 200 colleges and universities that are active members of the National Collegiate Athletic Association or belong to local athletic conferences that have allied membership in this

[3] U. S. Bureau of Education, Bulletin No. 5, *Physical Training in American Colleges*, 1885, p. 129.

[4] Alexander Johnston, "Football in the Eighties," *Century Magazine*, October, 1887, p. 898.

Association. The information sought was the total admissions at home football games and gross receipts from all football games between 1920 and 1930 together with the increase in seating facilities for spectators during this period. There was a commendable willingness to cooperate in this study but unfortunately few institutions have satisfactory records concerning football over a period of years. Replies either partial or complete were received from 135 institutions which comprise nearly two-thirds of the membership in the above Association and include all but a few of the large universities where football has for years received a large measure of public support.

The attendance at football games in 109 institutions reached a total of 5,538,661 during the season of 1930, which was 6 per cent less than the preceding year. One hundred and twenty-nine institutions reported that their football receipts during 1930 were $12,487,546, a million and a quarter dollars less than in 1929, a decline of 9 per cent. By dividing the institutions from which reports were received into 6 classes based on student enrollment, it was possible to compute the average attendance and receipts for each class and thus arrive at a fair estimate of the extent of public support of college football for the country as a whole. Computed in this way, the estimated total attendance at college football games during 1930 was approximately 10,300,000 while the total receipts amounted to $21,500,000.

It is interesting to note the extent to which public interest in football, as measured by attendance and receipts, is concentrated upon the larger universities. Nearly 60 per cent of the estimated attendance was at the games of about 40 institutions, each of which had a student enrollment of more than 3,500, although these universities constituted less than 10 per cent of the total number of institutions where football is played. Fourteen universities of more than 10,000 students each reported a total football attendance for 1930 of 1,868,326 or an average of 125,570 per school. The average gross receipts per school in 1930 ranged from

$5,565 for colleges of less than 500 students to $245,417 for universities of the largest size. Of the 129 colleges and universities reporting receipts for 1930, eight reported gross receipts of more than $500,000 each and 33 reported receipts of more than $100,000.

TABLE 23.—FOOTBALL ATTENDANCE AT 49 COLLEGES AND UNIVERSITIES CLASSIFIED BY GEOGRAPHICAL SECTIONS, 1921–1930[a]

Year	Northeast (19 reporting)	Middle West (18 reporting)	South (6 reporting)	West (6 reporting)	Total (49 reporting)
1921.............	928,225	475,679	33,900	66,515	1,504,319
1922.............	1,121,252	591,199	45,150	98,780	1,847,381
1923.............	1,144,949	755,298	44,300	138,848	2,083,395
1924.............	1,228,889	956,360	54,500	209,805	2,449,554
1925.............	1,255,721	963,002	65,700	260,800	2,545,223
1926.............	1,303,286	1,018,409	57,400	279,226	2,658,321
1927.............	1,459,166	1,224,812	62,700	306,299	3,052,977
1928.............	1,492,457	1,320,331	66,700	437,445	3,316,933
1929.............	1,719,793	1,404,012	69,100	424,516	3,617,421
1930.............	1,620,237	1,169,767	73,530	425,544	3,289,078

Index Number (1921 = 100)

Year	Northeast	Middle West	South	West	Total
1921.............	100	100	100	100	100
1922.............	121	124	133	135	123
1923.............	123	159	131	209	139
1924.............	132	201	161	315	163
1925.............	135	202	194	392	169
1926.............	140	214	169	420	177
1927.............	157	258	185	461	203
1928.............	161	278	197	658	221
1929.............	185	295	204	638	241
1930.............	175	246	217	640	219

[a] Compiled from data supplied by the colleges and universities.

The 49 institutions that reported their attendance for a ten year period more than doubled their admissions to games between 1921 and 1930, the increase being 119 per cent (Table 23). Football receipts, as reported by 65 institutions for this period, grew from $2,696,345 to $8,363,-674, a gain of 210 per cent (Table 24). Both attendance and receipts increased with considerable regularity during the first nine years of this period with a sharp falling off in 1930. While only a small number of institutions were able to give figures for the entire decade, the reliability of

TABLE 24.—FOOTBALL RECEIPTS IN 65 COLLEGES AND UNIVERSITIES, CLASSIFIED
BY GEOGRAPHICAL SECTIONS, 1921–1930[a]

Year	Northeast (22 reporting)	Middle West (27 reporting)	South (11 reporting)	West (5 reporting)	Total (65 reporting)
1921	1,669,589	712,706	204,149	109,901	2,696,345
1922	2,258,742	1,120,610	254,103	126,053	3,759,508
1923	2,242,854	1,256,246	262,704	164,143	3,925,947
1924	2,796,248	1,700,062	336,018	180,995	5,013,323
1925	2,888,431	1,890,244	416,233	251,574	5,446,482
1926	3,383,144	2,067,102	469,794	385,355	6,305,395
1927	3,824,675	2,534,970	563,942	543,800	7,467,387
1928	4,164,326	2,761,147	646,227	604,156	8,175,856
1929	4,489,783	2,943,848	783,523	815,006	9,032,160
1930	4,197,440	2,495,701	715,416	955,117	8,363,674

Index Number (1921 = 100)

Year	Northeast	Middle West	South	West	Total
1921	100	100	100	100	100
1922	135	157	125	115	139
1923	134	176	129	149	146
1924	168	239	165	165	186
1925	173	265	204	229	202
1926	203	290	230	351	234
1927	229	356	276	495	277
1928	249	387	317	550	303
1929	269	413	384	742	335
1930	251	350	350	869	310

[a] Compiled from data supplied by the colleges and universities.

the results is strengthened by the fact that it includes such
institutions as Harvard, Yale, Princeton, Pennsylvania,
New York, Illinois, Michigan, Northwestern, Ohio State,
and Southern California, all of which have played a prominent role in recent football history. Moreover, reports
for a five-year period, from 1926 to 1930, which were
received from 88 institutions on the matter of attendance
and from 102 institutions covering receipts, corroborate
in a striking manner the results secured for the full ten
year period. Figures from these institutions, which may be
regarded as fairly representative of the leading colleges
and universities, show that public support of college football increased steadily until the first year of the financial
depression, when attendance fell off 6 per cent and receipts
9 per cent (Table 26). Supplementary reports for the year
1931 from approximately 100 colleges and universities

show clearly that the curve of football attendance and receipts is continuing downward. The 1931 attendance at games was 8 per cent less than in 1930 while receipts fell off 4 per cent.[5] The general consensus is that this waning support of college football during 1930 and 1931 is due to hard times rather than to declining interest in the game as a public spectacle. Such an assumption seems reasonable in view of the fact that neither the curve of attendance nor of receipts showed any tendency to flatten out previous to 1930. A study of the reports from individual institutions shows no uniform falling off in receipts during the past two years. On the contrary, the most striking feature of the returns is the way in which the football losses of certain institutions are equalled by gains made by others. In spite of the depression football teams of championship caliber continued to attract capacity crowds and earn for their institutions greatly increased financial profits. As in professional baseball, the public shows no inclination to support a losing team and is not deterred by high prices nor hard times when a football championship is at stake.

The spectacular increase in attendance at football games during the past decade has been accompanied by an era of grandstand and stadium building far surpassing any previous developments of this kind. According to reports from 135 colleges and universities, the seating facilities for football spectators increased from 929,523 in 1920 to 2,307,850 in 1930, a gain of 148 per cent (Table 25). These institutions reported 74 concrete stadia, 55 of which had been erected between 1920 and 1930. Only one of these college stadia in 1920 had a seating capacity of more than 70,000 while there were seven in this class in 1930.

The building of the Harvard stadium in 1903 with a seating capacity of 23,500 set a pattern which was followed first in the northeastern states and then spread throughout the country. During the decade 1920–1930 the greatest advance in providing accommodations for football spec-

[5] For further evidence of the decline in gate receipts from college football see *Current Developments in American College Sport*, Bulletin No. 26, Carnegie Foundation for the Advancement of Teaching, 1931, p. 8.

tators was made in the Middle West, West, and South while the Northeast, where many stadia had previously been built, had the lowest rate of increase. This furnishes some evidence supporting the contention that the wave of college football enthusiasm is tending to die down in the Northeast and has been moving westward where it has already en-

TABLE 25.—SEATING CAPACITY OF COLLEGE STADIA AND STANDS, BY GEOGRAPHICAL SECTIONS, 1920 AND 1930[a]

Geographical section	Number of colleges reporting	Seating capacity		Increase	
		1920	1930	Number	Per cent
United States...............	135	929,523	2,307,850	1,378,327	148.3
Northeast...................	40	399,720	725,972	326,252	81.6
Middle West................	54	279,694	890,467	610,773	218.4
South......................	25	121,134	327,650	206,516	170.5
West.......................	16	128,975	363,761	234,786	182.0

[a] Compiled from data supplied by the colleges and universities.

gulfed most of the large universities and has led to enormous expenditures for stadia to accommodate the football crowds. This westward movement of football interest appears also in the fact that football receipts increased most rapidly in the West and South between 1926 and 1930 (Table 26). These sectional differences are much more striking for the entire decade, 1920–1930, but the number of institutions reporting for this period are too few to be fully representative of all sections of the country. With this limitation in mind it is interesting to note that college football receipts between 1920 and 1930 increased one and one-half times in northeastern colleges and universities, two and one-half times in the Middle West and South, and more than seven and one-half times in the West (Table 24).

Whatever may be the regional differences in the popularity of college football, it still has greater drawing power throughout the country as a whole than has any other college game. Students in general seem to take football less seriously than they were inclined to do ten years ago, but no other sport gives as great prestige to its successful participants. The huge investments in stadia which must be paid off in future years by successful football seasons make almost inevitable the continued approval of the

TABLE 26.—FOOTBALL RECEIPTS IN 102 COLLEGES AND UNIVERSITIES, CLASSIFIED BY GEOGRAPHICAL SECTIONS, 1926–1930[a]

Year	Northeast (33 reporting)	Middle West (40 reporting)	South (16 reporting)	West (13 reporting)	Total (102 reporting)
1926.............	$4,066,069	$2,884,169	$ 914,092	$1,328,879	$ 9,193,209
1927.............	4,522,953	3,359,071	1,048,384	1,589,785	10,520,193
1928.............	4,743,803	3,694,669	1,256,712	1,862,543	11,557,727
1929.............	5,405,626	3,805,884	1,427,783	2,111,209	12,750,502
1930.............	4,972,575	3,048,100	1,223,205	2,252,984	11,496,864

Index Number (1926 = 100)

1926.............	100	100	100	100	100
1927.............	111	116	114	119	114
1928.............	116	128	137	140	126
1929.............	133	132	157	159	135
1930.............	120	106	134	169	125

[a] Compiled from data supplied by the colleges and universities.

game by college administrative authorities. Its capacity to produce gate receipts and its value as an advertising medium cannot be ignored. Furthermore, the large increase in attendance at football games has little more than kept pace with student enrollment and the growing number of alumni. Football has shared in the general expansion of university activities and judged from this point of view is perhaps no more over-emphasized than it was during earlier years when the spectators were much fewer in number.

Nevertheless the criticisms of college football in its com-mercialized aspects are attracting wide attention and there is a growing feeling that college youth should not be exploited for the financial gain of the institution they represent. Already some of the colleges and universities have announced a reorganization of their athletic programs with less emphasis upon intercollegiate football. Student bodies are urging the adoption of an athletic policy that will give them wider opportunities for participation in the games of their choice. Many believe that college football as an entertainment enterprise is declining in popularity and that large crowds of spectators so common in the past will be found in the future only at some of the more important games. Apparently professional football, which has been making slow advances for the past thirty-five years, is now coming to the front and may eventually supplant the college game because of the superior skill of professional players. The 11 professional clubs of the National Football League have acquired secure status in the East and Middle West where their games are played and frequently attract crowds that range from 25,000 to 40,000 people.[6] As professional football develops throughout the country, public interest may shift from the college to the professional game as has been the case with college baseball, which continues to be a popular sport among college students without being a public spectacle.

Boxing and Prize Fighting.—Not until the closing years of last century did boxing gain legal status in this country and then only in a few states. The unsavory reputation of prize fighting because of its long history of brutality and the low type of men participating in it aroused widespread opposition to this sport and made it necessary to hold some of the early bouts in out of the way places or in frontier cities where there was little danger of police interference. Popular interest in boxing was considerably stimulated during the World War by its adoption in training camps as a sport well suited for the development of skill and hardihood among the soldiers. During the decade following the War boxing entered upon a period of growing popularity. Public opinion swung rapidly in favor of both professional and amateur boxing and important contests were held in New York, Philadelphia, Chicago, and a few other cities before record-breaking crowds. In 1930 twenty-

[6] F. G. Menke, *All Sports Record Book* (1932 edition), p. 157.

eight states had legalized the sport and placed it under control of officially appointed state athletic commissions. In the remaining states boxing still continues to be illegal or is permitted as exhibitions carried on under the auspices of private clubs.

When judged by attendance and more especially by receipts, the high tide of professional boxing was reached in 1926 and 1927 with the heavy weight championship bouts staged in Philadelphia and Chicago by Dempsey and Tunney. The attendance of 120,000 at the Philadelphia fight and the receipts amounting to $2,650,000 at the Chicago fight established new high records that have not yet been equalled. Other athletic sports have been able to draw large crowds but boxing stands first in its ability to produce large gate receipts at the more spectacular championship contests. At ten boxing matches held during the decade 1921–1930, the total gate receipts amounted to $11,468,496, an average of more than a million dollars at each bout. The extraordinary money raising capacity of this sport is a recent development for during the preceding decade the average of the highest gate receipts was less than $200,000 at each match and at the best patronized bouts held between 1901 and 1910 the average receipts were less than $60,000.

While few boxing contests since 1927 have attracted wide public interest, the sport still maintains a very considerable following in most of the large cities. The total number of boxing matches in Connecticut, Idaho, Illinois, Kansas, Michigan, and North Carolina, according to information furnished by the State Athletic Commissions of those states, increased steadily between 1926 and 1930 and the attendance continued to mount upward until 1930 when there was a sharp decline. The high point in the receipts was reached in 1927 because of the Dempsey-Tunney fight in Chicago. With this exception the receipts also tend to expand each year, with a decrease of 27 per cent in 1930 (Table 27). Further indication of the recent downward trend is seen in the declining federal taxes collected

[95]

from this source. In 1929, the first year that receipts from boxing matches were reported separately by the Commissioner of Internal Revenue, the taxes amounted to $398,132. In 1931 the receipts from this source were $265,023, a decline of 33 per cent during this two year period. In spite of this declining public support, professional boxing bouts are still sufficiently popular to make this sport profitable for those engaged in its promotion. The most recent evidence of this was the championship bout

TABLE 27.—ATTENDANCE AND RECEIPTS AT PROFESSIONAL BOXING BOUTS HELD IN CONNECTICUT, IDAHO, ILLINOIS, KANSAS, MICHIGAN, AND NORTH CAROLINA, 1926–1930[a]

Year	Number of bouts	Attendance	Receipts
1926	459	449,346	$ 875,759
1927	488	755,191	3,623,668
1928	575	827,832	1,382,950
1929	650	904,189	1,818,971
1930	727	845,306	1,315,732

[a] Compiled from data supplied by the State Athletic Commissions of the above states.

between Schmeling and Sharkey in Madison Square Garden Bowl, New York, in 1932. Seventy thousand people paid $500,000 to see this fight, and by means of a nation-wide radio broadcast fight fans all over the country were able to follow it round by round.[7]

One indication that boxing is gaining a higher status as an athletic sport is the growing interest in amateur boxing sponsored by college and other athletic associations. Many colleges maintain boxing teams with a regular schedule of intercollegiate and intramural contests. The Golden Gloves Amateur boxing contest sponsored by the Chicago *Daily Tribune* and the New York *Daily News* for the past few years has greatly stimulated the development of skill in boxing and has demonstrated that the sport can draw large crowds when conducted as a boxing match and not as a prize fight. At the finals of this tournament

[7] *Literary Digest*, July 2, 1932, p. 38.

held in the Chicago Stadium in 1931 the paid admissions were 23,000.[8]

Professional boxing, however, in spite of control by state athletic commissions, has failed to free itself entirely from the undesirable associations that have so long clung to it. Boxing more than any other sport has been exploited for purposes of excessive financial gain by both its promoters and participants. Its fascination for many people consists in the fact that it is a bodily combat with serious risks of physical injury. Some of the most popular boxers have been sluggers capable of giving and taking a large amount of punishment. It is this aspect of professional boxing that makes possible the high prices of admission to championship fights but it prevents this sport from making much headway in winning complete public approval.

Athletic Sports and Publicity Devices.—The role of athletic sports in providing passive amusement for the nation cannot be fully determined by counting the spectators at games and contests. An important leisure-time activity of unnumbered thousands is reading the sport pages of newspapers and listening to the radio broadcast of games in which they are interested. The growth of popular interest in athletic sports as an amusement enterprise is reflected in the remarkable increase in the amount of space given by newspapers to sport news concerned primarily with records and championships and day by day victories and defeats of teams and individual athletes. The sports section has become a regular feature of the daily press and in some of the afternoon papers reports of important games are given space on the first page. This increased emphasis upon sport news has gone along with the expansion of other departments of the newspaper but in general the space given to sports has tended to show the most rapid growth.

In connection with the recent report on college athletics by the Carnegie Foundation, a study was made of the sports pages in six daily newspapers, the New York *Sun*, New

[8] F. G. Menke, *All Sports Record Book* (1932 edition), p. 112.

York *Times*, New York *World*, Boston *Transcript*, Salt Lake *Deseret News*, and San Francisco *Chronicle*. In the three New York newspapers the sports news increased 167 per cent between the years 1913 and 1927. The proportion of space given the sports news, however, remained about the same, being approximately 10 per cent of the total news space for the two years studied. During these fourteen years the space given to school and college athletics made the greatest gain with an increase of 245 per cent while the space given to professional sports increased 110 per cent. In the remaining three papers the sports space advanced 112 per cent with school and college athletics occupying a place of growing importance during this period until in 1927 they were given more than three times the space accorded to professional athletics.[9]

Between 1920 and 1930 the amount of space given to sports in the Chicago *Tribune* showed a gain of 79 per cent while the total news space increased 76 per cent. Amusements occupied less actual space than athletic sports but increased their amount of space 229 per cent during this ten year period, largely because of the greater attention given to the movies and the radio. The percentage of total news space given to sports remained approximately the same in 1920 and in 1930 but in the case of amusements the proportion was twice as great in 1930 as it was ten years previously. The popularity of football is seen in the fact that the space given this sport increased 145 per cent while the space given to baseball advanced but 23 per cent (Table 28).

In the study of Middletown it was found that organized sports showed "a greater increase since 1890 in the relative amount of news space devoted to them in the Middletown press than any other department of news—from 4 per cent of the total news content of the leading paper in 1890 to 16 per cent in 1923. For the three sample months of January, July, and October, 1923, the leading paper mentioned 169,

[9] H. J. Savage, *American College Athletics*, Bulletin No. 23, Carnegie Foundation for the Advancement of Teaching, New York, 1929, pp. 267–272.

70, and 98 organized and unorganized sporting and athletic events in the city as against 6, 15, and 7 for the corresponding months of 1890."[10]

Even weekly newspapers, which cater largely to rural and small town readers, are more and more following the example of the city dailies in giving greater emphasis to athletic sports. A recent study of Minnesota weekly newspapers showed that while only a small percentage of the news space is utilized for sports news, events in the world of

TABLE 28.—NEWS SPACE GIVEN TO ATHLETIC SPORTS AND AMUSEMENTS IN CHICAGO DAILY AND SUNDAY *Tribune*, 1920 AND 1930[a]

Class of news	1920 (column inches)	1930 (column inches)	Per cent increase
Total news space....................	77,388	136,953	76
Total athletic sports.................	6,849	12,273	79
Total amusements...................	2,494	8,217	229
Baseball.........................	2,149	2,639	23
Football.........................	948	2,323	145
Moving pictures...................	450	1,957	335
Radio broadcasting...............	......	1,743	

[a] Based on special study made in connection with the preparation of this volume. The sample comprises the first Sunday and first Wednesday issues of each month.

sport are being reported much more frequently, especially since 1920. The average number of column inches of shop-set sport news increased from 3.23 in 1900 to 14.23 in 1929 and the proportion of shop-set news space given to sports increased during this period from 1.80 to 3.68.[11] To a far greater extent than ever before people living in the more isolated places where there is no opportunity to witness important athletic events keep in touch with the fortunes of rival athletic teams and discuss in their hours of leisure the achievements of their favorite players.

Recently this detailed reporting of athletic sports and games has been supplemented and made far more vivid by radio broadcasting. It is now common practice for local

[10] Robert S. Lynd and Helen M. Lynd, *Middletown*, New York, 1929, p. 284.
[11] Irene Barnes Taeuber, *Changes in the Content and Presentation of Reading in Minnesota Weekly Newspapers, 1860–1929* (Unpublished thesis).

broadcasting stations to describe play by play many of the baseball, football, and basketball games played within their city and for championship events of wide interest to be brought within reach of the entire country by means of a nation-wide hook-up of radio stations. With 40 per cent of all families in this country owning radios, this potential unseen radio audience has become exceedingly large, far outnumbering those who can crowd into the field where the game is being played. Through the development of radio the role of athletic sports as a means for passive entertainment has been multiplied many fold. Listening to radio accounts of games has become a leisure-time activity of real importance and will likely assume greater proportions in the future if it continues to be profitable to advertise athletic sports in this manner.

Spectatorism versus Participation.—Since the World War the extraordinary public interest in commercialized sports and amusements has led to a rather widespread belief that Americans prefer to be amused by others rather than to participate actively in sports and games. There can be no doubt that opportunities to enjoy passive amusements have in recent years become both more numerous and attractive. Moving pictures during the past decade have been greatly improved. Athletic games and contests may be no more interesting than formerly but great advance has been made in providing comfortable and commodious seating facilities for spectators. Those who do not wish to venture forth from their own homes can through the radio follow the progress of important games and enjoy a wide variety of entertainment. Under these circumstances it is inevitable that passive amusements should form a very considerable part of our leisure-time activities.

While huger crowds assemble to witness sports and amusements than was customary a decade or two ago, this growth of spectatorism has been a part of the growth of cities and has been paralleled by advances made in many other lines. The building of large stadia, and the expansion of other facilities for passive amusements have been accompanied by increased acreage of public parks, and by a rapidly growing number of athletic fields, golf courses, tennis courts, swimming pools, and bathing beaches constructed for the use of the mass of the people. The crowds that fill the baseball and football stadia are apparently matched, although in a less spectacular way, by the hundreds of thousands of golf and tennis enthusiasts and by the large numbers of people who throng the municipal bathing beaches.

As a matter of fact, in the development of American athletic sports, the two roles of participant and observer have been combined in a very effective manner. The profits from college football have in many instances been utilized in building up a comprehensive system of intramural athletics. Attendance at professional games has stimulated interest in outdoor sports and aided in developing a public opinion that has insisted upon municipal appropriations for playing fields for the people. Grandstands and stadia for spectators represent the most economical use of space for the enjoyment of sports and make possible wholesome entertainment for the many thousands who for various reasons cannot participate actively in sports and games.

In spite of the fact that many people spend much of their leisure in watching others play, it is noteworthy that it is becoming difficult to get public support of games where championships are not at stake or where widely known and popular players do not participate. The major league baseball parks are crowded to full capacity during the world series but the teams that fall behind during the playing season do not attract many spectators. The curve of football attendance at any university rises and falls each year depending upon the quality of the team and its chance of winning a championship. A certain number of people may attend games simply because of their interest in watching a contest, but the large crowds are found only at important games to which wide publicity has been given by the newspaper press. The most striking fact about athletic sports today is not the cheering crowds on the sidelines but the large numbers of players, both young and old and men and women, who are eager to improve their own game in competition with their fellows. In view of the insistent and growing demand for greater opportunities to participate in athletic sports and games, it seems absurd to maintain that Americans are becoming a nation of spectators.

CHAPTER VI

TRENDS IN COMMERCIAL AMUSEMENTS

THE business of providing entertainment and diversions for the people has never faced such serious competition as at the present time and yet remains more widely extended and profitable than ever before. So great has become the demand for recreational opportunities and facilities of various kinds that even the great expansion of private recreational clubs supplemented by the government's entrance into the field of recreation has been entirely inadequate to deal with this problem. Business enterprise has been quick to take advantage of this situation and expand its amusement facilities wherever there was opportunity for financial profit. This provision of recreation on a commercial basis is as legitimate and inevitable as is the supply of food and other articles required in daily living. At present as in the past commercial interests are in control of many different forms of amusements and their position has become more firmly entrenched both by increasing patronage and by greater efficiency in business organization. The total amount of recreation that is made available on this commercial basis is enormous and provides for a very considerable share of the leisure time of the mass of the people. In this field, as in the other phases of recreation, satisfactory data for the measuring of trends are not completely available, but it is possible to indicate some of the more significant changes that are occurring.

Commercialization in the Field of Sports.—The widespread interest of the public in games and sports has made this type of recreation a very lucrative one for those engaged in exploiting it for financial gain. The preceding chapter has already pointed out the large expenditures of the American public to see baseball and football games and boxing con-

[103]

tests. Baseball has become so thoroughly commercialized that it is operated as a big business with its leading players practically all professionals who devote their whole time to the game during the playing season. In spite of the increasing competition with other forms of sport, professional baseball still remains popular with the public and continues to be a profitable business undertaking for many of its promoters. College football is played by men who maintain their amateur standing but the huge investments in grandstands and stadia, the efforts made to attract large crowds, the high prices charged for admission, and the large profits in many instances at the end of the playing season, make it clearly evident that the game is dominated by the commercial spirit even though not promoted by commercial interests. Recently professional football teams, made up largely of former college players, have gained a considerable following in some of the large cities and very probably mark the beginning of the further commercialization of this popular sport. Prize fighting has had a long history as a commercialized sport and during the decade 1920–1930 earned record making purses for the more successful boxers and their promoters. Wrestling, ice hockey, basket ball, tennis, and even golf are other athletic sports which have produced professional players whose skill has been utilized in public contests and exhibitions for the making of money.

Racing is another form of sport so widely popular that it has proved to be a profitable field for financial exploitation. Horse racing since colonial days has been a prominent American sport with peculiar capacity to attract large crowds of people. The trotting or harness races have long been one of the important entertainment features of county and state fairs and other agricultural exhibitions and continue their wide vogue in spite of the fact that betting is usually prohibited. About a thousand race meets of this kind are held in the United States each year.[1] The thoroughbred or running races, which attract far more public in-

[1] Article on "Horse Racing," Encyclopaedia Britannica, 14th Edition, Vol. 2: 770.

terest, have had a checkered career because of their close association with gambling and have from time to time been abolished in different states by hostile legislation. The chief running tracks in this country at present are located in about two dozen places in the states of Illinois, Kentucky, Louisiana, Maryland, Nevada, and New York. The attend-

TABLE 29.—RECEIPTS FOR ADMISSION TO MARYLAND RACE TRACKS AND AMOUNT OF PARI-MUTUEL WAGERS, 1925–1930[a]

Year	Receipts for admission	Pari-mutuel wagers
1925....................	$1,072,972	$54,375,264
1927....................	1,108,589	53,794,707
1929....................	1,199,851	54,419,867
1930....................	1,103,194	47,754,676

[a] Compiled from Annual Reports of the Maryland Racing Commission.

ance at the races in Illinois increased from 420,295 in 1927, the year when racing was legalized in this state, to 776,510 in 1930.[2] In 1925 the amount paid for admission to the Maryland race tracks totaled $1,072,972 while in 1930 it had increased to $1,103,194 (Table 29). The growing interest in racing as well as the larger number of races can be

TABLE 30.—TOTAL PURSES AND STAKES ON RUNNING RACE TRACKS, 1912–1930[a]

Year	Total purses	Year	Total purses
1912....................	$2,391,625	1922....................	$ 9,096,215
1914....................	2,994,525	1924....................	10,825,446
1916....................	3,842,471	1926....................	13,884,820
1918....................	3,425,347	1928....................	13,332,361
1920....................	7,773,407	1930....................	13,674,160

[a] F. G. Menke, *All Sports Record Book* (1932 edition), p. 205. Figures for Canadian, Mexican, and Cuban tracks also included.

inferred from the fact that the total money paid to winning owners of horses by race tracks in the United States, Canada, Mexico, and Cuba increased from $7,773,407 to $13,674,160 between the years 1920 and 1930 (Table 30). Horse racing takes on added significance from the point of

[2] Information furnished by the Illinois State Department of Agriculture.

view of the cost of recreation because of the large amounts of money that change hands on wagers. It has been estimated that the yearly total of betting at race tracks in the United States, Canada, and Mexico is $450,000,000.[3] This estimate does not seem excessive in view of the fact that during 92 days of racing at the Maryland tracks in 1930, $47,754,676 passed through the pari-mutuel machines in addition to the unknown amount that was wagered in other ways (Table 29).

Dog races with a mechanical rabbit as the object of pursuit, six-day bicycle races, and automobile speedway races are other types of racing promoted for financial profit. Such races are frequently given much attention by the newspaper press and attract large crowds but they have not spread widely through the country and therefore are not of great importance as commercial amusements.

Among the indoor games that have been exploited by commercial interests, pool, billiards, and bowling are perhaps the most important. Computed from federal taxes paid by commercial establishments operating these games, the number of tables and alleys in 1900 was 73,346. By the year 1915 they had more than doubled, the number being 158,-282, and five years later they had increased to 278,216. Beginning with 1921 a decline in these sports set in, and in 1926, the last year that federal taxes were paid, they numbered only 171,466, a decrease of 62 per cent since 1920 (Table 31). In Chicago the number of pool and billiard halls and the number of tables approximately doubled between 1910 and 1920 while during the following decade the number of halls fell off two-thirds and the tables declined 40 per cent. The number of bowling alleys, however, more than doubled during the past decade with a slight decrease in the number of amusement places operating these alleys. In Indiana between 1916–1917 and 1928–1929, there was a gain of 18 per cent in the number of pool and billiard halls but the average number of halls per city declined for each class of cities above 2,500 population. Apparently the nation-wide decline

[3] New York *World*, October 12, 1930.

in these sports has proceeded very unevenly because of various influences. The unsavory reputation of many commercial pool halls caused by their close association with gambling interests is undoubtedly responsible for their retarded growth in many places. In cities where public recreation facilities have made rapid progress, pool halls have frequently found it difficult to compete with the increased opportunities for various kinds of recreation. The present trend seems to be away from the small, ill-kept hall with

TABLE 31.—NUMBER AND VALUE OF POOL AND BILLIARD TABLES AND BOWLING ALLEYS, 1919–1929

Year	Number[a]	Value[b]	Year	Number[a]	Value[b]
1919	161,198	$15,733,047	1924	231,281	
1920	278,216		1925	228,983	$5,614,319
1921	236,800	7,367,920	1926	171,466	
1922	249,983		1927	....	7,111,871
1923	237,109	6,236,394	1929	....	8,821,363

[a] Computed from receipts from the federal tax on pool and billiard tables and bowling alleys, Annual Reports of the United States Commissioner of Internal Revenue. Tables and alleys have not been taxed since 1926.

[b] *United States Census of Manufactures,* 1929.

one or two tables to large, centrally located halls equipped and supervised in a manner designed to appeal to a better clientele. The bowling alleys have been especially successful in breaking away from many of their earlier undesirable associations and now occupy a much higher status. Nevertheless, in spite of improved conditions in many instances, these commercial amusement centers are frequently headquarters for race track and baseball pools and attract among their patrons many who are chiefly interested in their betting and gaming devices.

The commercialization of sport can be still further seen in the opportunities presented to popular athletes and winners of championships to capitalize their fame by starring in moving pictures, appearing in vaudeville skits, giving endorsements of commodities, or engaging in professional exhibitions of their skill. The financial rewards that may be secured by athletes during the height of their fame are greater than ever before and are made possible by the wide publicity in the sports pages of newspapers which make their names household words throughout the nation. After the amateur sportsman of the present day has won his cups and medals, it is taken for granted that he will sacrifice his amateur status for financial gain. Not all respond to this lure of gold but the public looks with toleration if not with full approval upon this growing tendency to commercialize fame and skill in the field of sports.

Commercialized Dramatic Amusements.—The drama, which has long been a favorite field for exploitation by commercial interests, has attained a new importance as a popular form of entertainment during the past quarter century through the spectacular development of the motion picture. The legitimate stage, vaudeville, burlesque, dime museums, chautauquas, and penny arcades have all been forced into the background by this modern amusement device with its almost universal appeal to the mass of the people. Beginning with short reels that were used to fill out a vaudeville program, the motion picture gradually improved its technique until it became the principal attraction and could furnish a complete show of its own. The typical motion picture theater during the first years of this century was a store show room and the equipment needed was of the simplest kind—a screen, chairs for the spectators, and a pianist to provide the music. In 1907 the nickelodeons, as the first moving picture theaters were called, numbered approximately 5,000, and in spite of the crudity of many of the films were beginning to play a prominent role in the world of amusement.[4] The possibilities of the silent screen became evident with the production of *The Birth of The Nation* in 1915 and the whole moving picture industry went forward with increasing rapidity. The unattractive halls in which the earlier pictures were shown were superseded by specially constructed theaters of larger size. The past decade has been an era of "million dollar movie palaces" erected in practically all the large cities. Everywhere the

[4] M. R. Davie, *Problems of City Life*, 1932, p. 573.

recent tendency has been to build large well-located theaters which have forced out of business many of the smaller neighborhood theaters which once enjoyed wide patronage. During recent years the number of theaters has shown a marked decline but the number of seats has greatly increased. The number of moving picture theaters with a seating capacity of 2,000 or more increased in Chicago between 1915 and 1930 from none to 30 while those with

TABLE 32.—NUMBER OF MOTION PICTURE THEATERS AND POPULATION PER THEATER, BY GEOGRAPHICAL DIVISIONS, 1929

Geographical division	Number of theaters[a]	Population per theater	Geographical division	Number of theaters[a]	Population per theater
United States.........	23,938	5,129	South Atlantic.......	2,440	6,473
			East South Central...	1,297	7,623
New England.........	1,330	6,140	West South Central..	2,204	5,525
Middle Atlantic.......	3,665	7,165	Mountain...........	1,283	2,885
East North Central...	4,929	5,132	Pacific.............	1,687	4,857
West North Central...	5,103	2,606			

[a] Compiled from a list of theaters given in the Film Year Book, 1929.

accommodations for less than 500 declined in number approximately 300 per cent. In Seattle between 1920 and 1930 the number of theaters declined from 61 to 47 and their total seating capacity grew from 30,830, to 39,767.

In January, 1931, there were 22,731 motion picture theaters in this country with a seating capacity of approximately 11,300,000. The motion picture industry represents an investment of more than two billion dollars; its annual expenditures, exclusive of advertising, rose from $77,000,-000 in 1921 to $184,000,000 in 1929 (Table 33). The total weekly attendance at motion picture theaters in 1930 was between 100 million and 115 million and the amount spent for admissions was at least one and a half billion dollars.[5]

A striking characteristic of the whole moving picture industry has been its aggressiveness in making new improvements regardless of expense. The installation of sound equipment has already cost more than $500,000,000.

[5] Estimates made by the National Association of Motion Picture Producers and Distributors of America, Inc.

A number of elaborate feature films have each cost between one and two million dollars to produce. Vaudeville programs and excellent orchestras are among the devices used to increase attendance when interest in the pictures seems to be declining. Elaborately equipped theaters well designed for their purpose have been provided to give a proper setting for the films. The modern theaters of the best

TABLE 33.—COST OF PRODUCTION OF MOTION PICTURE FILMS, 1921-1929[a]

Year	Cost of production	Index number (1921 = 100)
1921	$ 77,397,381	100
1923	86,418,170	112
1925	93,636,348	121
1927	134,343,360	174
1929	184,102,419	238

[a] *United States Census of Manufactures.*

type are adorned with tapestries, fountains, fine statuary and paintings, attendants are dressed in attractive liveries, appropriate music is provided, and careful attention is given to every detail that would reinforce the illusion of the screen and enable the spectator to live for awhile in a world far removed from the routine of daily life. Along with this development of fine surroundings, there has been built up an extensive campaign of publicity which has kept the moving picture stars before the public and aroused widespread interest in new films about to be released. The wide vogue of moving pictures is at least partially a result of well planned, continuous advertising.

The advent of sound pictures during the past few years represents a revolutionary change which has greatly stimulated public interest and made possible a further expansion of the motion picture industry. Between 1926 and 1930 the attendance at motion picture theaters was 75 per cent greater than during the preceding five-year period, an upward trend due in large measure to the installation of sound and talking equipment. At the end of 1931 the theaters wired for sound numbered 14,805, about three-fourths of the total number operating at that time.[6]

When the moving picture was first introduced, five cents was the usual admission price. Gradually as the cost of producing films increased and more palatial theaters were built, the tickets advanced in price until their average cost increased six or eight times beyond the original figure. Nevertheless, the price of admission has always remained far below that of the legitimate stage and today as in the past the moving picture remains a low-priced form of entertainment well within the reach of the mass of the people.

While the moving picture has become the most popular and widespread form of dramatic entertainment, it has had to make its way in the face of much serious criticism. Many believe that its vivid portrayal of scenes in which suggestive situations, questionable conduct, and crime frequently play a prominent role presents a false and exaggerated view of life and may even be a positive menace to morals. There can be no doubt that some of the films have been vulgar, demoralizing and even criminally suggestive. On the other hand, some of the most popular and successful films have been of an exceedingly high order of art and are wholesome from every point of view. No adequate measure of the quality of moving pictures is available and therefore it is difficult to judge whether their standards show an upward or downward trend. It is generally agreed that official censorship has not been a satisfactory means of dealing with the situation. The National Association of Motion Picture Producers and Distributors, while under the necessity of catering to popular taste so as to insure financial profit, has vigorously asserted its purpose of building up high moral and artistic standards within the industry. The future trends in film production, as far as questions of morals are concerned, will doubtless be determined by public opinion which is gradually becom-

[6] From data supplied by the National Association of Motion Picture Producers and Distributors of America, Inc.

ing more effectively organized in the interests of a more wholesome form of entertainment.

Twenty years ago when the moving picture had gained wide popularity, it was predicted that vaudeville and burlesque, which had long been furnishing popular entertainment at low prices, would soon be forced out of business. To a large degree this prediction has come true, for these older forms of entertainment have either been supplanted or driven into a position of secondary importance. Vaudeville shows, which formerly introduced the public to motion pictures by inserting a short film between their regular acts, now find their position reversed and must be content with short stage presentations between showings of the feature film. This device of combining moving pictures with stage shows of the vaudeville type was widely used by moving picture theater owners during the years immediately preceding the advent of the sound and talking pictures and proved to be very successful in the large houses that were equipped with a stage and could afford this additional expense. Vaudeville theaters of the earlier type, in which the chief emphasis is upon the stage show consisting of a series of dancing, musical, and acrobatic acts, are now seldom found outside of the largest cities. Another type of stage show that still persists in some cities is the cheap musical comedy and burlesque show located on the fringe of white light districts and catering either to male audiences or to a low class of patrons. Shows of this kind in which sex appeal is their main reliance flourish most in areas occupied by homeless men and apparently have lost none of their popularity among those who seek that form of entertainment.

Commercial Dance Halls.—The provision of facilities for dancing has long been a profitable field for commercial exploitation. Prior to the enactment of the federal prohibition law, saloon keepers frequently maintained a large hall adjacent to their premises, which was utilized for both public and private dances, their profits coming largely from the sale of liquor to the participants. Later, independently operated halls with a minimum of equipment and often poorly supervised came into existence and proved to be successful business ventures. More recently it has been found profitable to operate well equipped ball rooms in which dances open to the public are held each night with music furnished by a popular orchestra that may broadcast its numbers while the dance is in progress. With the development of these so-called dance palaces capable of accommodating several thousands of people, the small, unattractive hall is becoming less common. In Chicago commercial dance halls declined from 315 in 1910 to 225 in 1930 while their total capacity greatly increased. This tendency toward a decline in numbers and increase in size seems to be quite general throughout the country among the halls that solicit general patronage. Dance halls of this kind are usually well located in down town areas or in sub-business districts where they are easily accessible and efforts are made by their management to maintain standards of conduct that would not be offensive to the better class of people.

Of a quite different type are the closed or taxi-dance halls which cater only to male patronage. Such halls employ their own girls who serve as dance partners for the patrons on a commission basis. Tickets for each dance usually sell for ten cents, half of which goes to the girl who is chosen by the patron as his partner. Some of the smaller dance halls in the larger cities, unable to compete with the more elaborate ball rooms, adopted this new method of operation in an effort to save themselves from extinction. It was during the post-war period that dance halls of this type became sufficiently numerous to attract much public attention. Their rapid spread in practically all the large cities during the past decade gives some indication of their popularity among the groups from which their patrons are drawn.[7] The commercialization of the dance appears in its most extreme form in the closed dance hall and it presents problems of supervision and control that have not yet been successfully met.

[7] Paul G. Cressey, *The Taxi-Dance Hall*, University of Chicago Press, Chicago, 1932, ch. 2.

[113]

Other commercial auspices which seek financial profits by providing facilities for dancing are dancing academies, dine-and-dance restaurants, hotels, cabarets, night clubs, roadhouses, and excursion boats. While all these establishments are extensively patronized by those seeking opportunities to dance, it is no longer as necessary as it was formerly to rely upon such institutions for facilities for this form of entertainment. Community centers, field houses in public parks, country clubs and other private clubs, and innumerable homes equipped with the radio provide many opportunities for social dancing. Commercial dance halls face keen competition not merely with other facilities for dancing but with a large variety of sports and amusements that are now more accessible to young people than ever before.

Cabarets, Night Clubs, Roadhouses.—Commercial amusement places of this general class differ widely in many particulars but may be grouped together because of their common tendency to combine the dispensing of food and drink, usually at exorbitant prices, with some form of entertainment provided by the establishment and informally participated in by the patrons. The cabaret's specialty has been vaudeville acts or musical revues provided for the entertainment of the guests while the latter are partaking of refreshments. With the coming of prohibition the cabarets have tended to merge into so-called night clubs where liquor has become an added lure along with the other attractions of such resorts. These night clubs, which are clubs only in name since their doors are open to bona fide customers, are of many different kinds ranging from places where patrons may dine and dance to resorts of ill-repute closely associated with the activities of the underworld. During the past decade the wide use of the automobile has brought into existence roadhouses located along the highways outside of large cities. These amusement places play a role similar to that of the night clubs and have an added attraction to many people since they are free from the surveillance of city law enforcement agencies thus making it possible for their patrons to determine their own standards of conduct.

Whether commercial amusement places of this general type are increasing or decreasing in numbers cannot be accurately determined because of the lack of statistical data. The most comprehensive measure, which is obviously incomplete, is the federal taxes listed by the Commissioner of Internal Revenue under the heading, roof gardens, cabarets, etc. In 1921 these taxes amounted to $790,925 while in 1931 they totaled only $507,983, a decline of about 35 per cent. Between these years the tax receipts varied irregularly but they failed to reach the high level attained in 1921 (Table 34). Eighty-seven per cent of the

TABLE 34.—RECEIPTS FROM THE FEDERAL TAX ON ROOF GARDENS, CABARETS, ETC., 1920–1931[a]

Year	Receipts	Year	Receipts
1920...........................	$498,822	1926...........................	$703,793
1921...........................	790,925	1927...........................	715,746
1922...........................	599,800	1928...........................	714,863
1923...........................	659,865	1929...........................	664,077
1924...........................	701,486	1930...........................	711,752
1925...........................	634,216	1931...........................	507,983

[a] Annual Reports of the United States Commissioner of Internal Revenue.

federal taxes paid by such establishments were collected in five states—California, Illinois, Massachusetts, New York, and Pennsylvania—which indicates a marked concentration of these places of entertainment in the largest cities. New York alone paid slightly less than half of these taxes in 1931. In 1921 these taxes were collected in 28 states while in 1931 the states in which such taxes were paid had decreased to 22.[8] The conclusion is apparently justified that the amusement places of this class which pay taxes to the federal government have declined during the past decade. It is probable, however, that this form of commercial entertainment has become more widely prevalent

[8] Annual Reports of the United States Commissioner of Internal Revenue.

during recent years because of the many road houses and similar resorts that have appeared in the vicinity of both small and large cities in all parts of the country.

Amusement Parks.—The commercially operated amusement park, as it has developed in America, has attained considerable popularity as a place of entertainment for city people during the summer months. Its widely renowned prototype, Coney Island, which still stands first among enterprises of this kind, has for many years been New York City's most popular resort and has served as the model or pattern for many similar places of amusement elsewhere. The total daily attendance at Coney Island on its most crowded days during the summer months is estimated to be 800,000 with at least half a million people on its grounds at one time.[9] Following the World War a National Association of Amusement Parks was organized and there began an expansion of the amusement park industry which brought about their establishment in many cities throughout the entire country. During recent years a large number of these resorts have been closed, especially in the smaller cities, but they still remain a paying investment in the large urban centers and in the localities where summer visitors congregate. The entertainment features of these parks consist of ferris wheels, merry-go-rounds, scenic panoramas, high diving, roller skating, dancing, shooting galleries, penny arcades, side shows of various kinds, and gambling or quasi-gambling devices of infinite variety. Their emphasis is upon exhilarating and sensational types of amusement and efforts are made to promote the carnival spirit and encourage the free spending of money. Amusement places of this kind, in spite of the competition with public parks with their facilities for wholesome outdoor games, still possess great drawing power and provide recreation for large numbers of people.

Traveling Chautauquas.—Although offering a different kind of entertainment from the amusement park, the travel-

[9] Lee F. Hanmer, *Public Recreation*, p. 116, Regional Survey of New York and its Environs, Vol. 5, New York, 1928.

ing chautauqua, at the height of its development, occupied a prominent place in the field of commercialized recreation. Taking its pattern from the earlier Chautauqua and Lyceum movements, this enterprise, which first got under way early in the present century, organized troupes of speakers, musicians, and other entertainers who traveled from town to town according to a prearranged schedule and gave standardized programs lasting from a few days to a week. The Chautauqua Bureaus, under whose auspices these programs were developed, provided the equipment, consisting of tents, seats, etc., employed the personnel, furnished transportation, and made the financial arrangements with the cities and towns that made up the circuit. A chautauqua giving a five day's program had five sets of tents and played in five towns simultaneously. By dividing the entertainers into five sections, each giving a day's program in one town and then moving on, an endless chain was put in motion which gave continuous employment to all and greatly reduced the operating expenses. Through this plan of organization, a town could secure a week's entertainment for one or two thousand dollars depending upon the kind of program selected.

The traveling chautauqua gained its greatest foothold in the towns and small cities where there was little competition with other forms of amusement. In many places chautauqua week, during its years of greatest popularity, became a gala occasion. Visitors came from miles around, many bringing their tents and camping outfit. Merchants closed their stores and all local programs were postponed while the chautauqua was in progress.

The traveling chautauqua reached its peak during and immediately following the years of the World War when there were at least 12,000 American and Canadian towns and cities included in the circuits of the various Bureaus with an estimated annual attendance of more than 20,000,-000 people. During the past decade the movement has shown a marked decline. In 1930 it was estimated that there were less than 10 per cent as many towns with an annual chautauqua as there were ten years before.[10] The automobile, the motion picture, and the radio are new attractions with which the chautauqua has not been able to compete. Apparently the last stronghold of this form of entertainment is the small agricultural town with a population of 1,500 or less. Even in these isolated places it is becoming increasingly difficult to secure sufficient public support to make this enterprise financially profitable to its promoters.

Radio Broadcasting.—Radio programs, which now play a large role in the field of recreation, have been developed and are still conducted in this country by commercial interests and therefore belong in the class of commercial amusements. This form of entertainment was first made available to the American public in 1920 when the Westinghouse Electric and Manufacturing Company established station KDKA and began the transmission of regular programs. Other cities followed this example and the number of broadcasting stations grew in number until in 1930 there were 612 located in all sections of the country.[11] Meanwhile the manufacture of radio receiving sets went forward rapidly and grew to remarkable proportions. In 1921, according to the Census of Manufactures, the value of radio apparatus manufactured that year amounted to $11,745,585. Four years later the value at the factory of such goods had increased to $150,046,130. Between 1925 and 1929 their value had more than doubled, the amount for the latter year being $411,637,312 (Table 35). These figures of course do not represent the cost of radio to the consumer. The retail radio sales during 1929, according to the 1930 edition of the American Year Book, amounted to $842,548,000. The following year sales fell off more than 40 per cent with a still further decline in 1931, partly because of the financial depression and partly because of

[10] G. S. Dalgety, "Chautauqua's Contribution to American Life," *Current History*, April, 1931, pp. 39–44. J. S. Noffsinger, *Correspondence Schools, Lyceums, Chautauquas*, pp. 126, 142.
[11] President's Research Committee on Social Trends, *Recent Social Trends in the United States*, Chapter IV.

lower prices and the growing popularity of midget sets.[12] The number of families having radio sets, according to the 1930 census, was 12,078,345. Within the short space of ten years 40 per cent of all families in this country were equipped with radios, a rate of growth that gives some indication of the wide popularity of this form of entertainment.

TABLE 35.—VALUE OF RADIO APPARATUS, 1921–1929

Year	Value[a] (at factory)	Index number (1921 = 100)
1921	$ 11,745,585	100
1923	29,678,548	253
1925	150,046,130	1,278
1927	149,657,894	1,274
1929	411,637,312	3,505

a United States Census of Manufactures.

This enormous expansion of the radio industry has been made possible because of the wide appeal of its entertainment features. At first it was regarded largely as a novelty and many radio fans spent their leisure time constructing home-made sets and trying to get distant stations. Reception was not always good and only the best receiving sets could bring in satisfactorily the more attractive programs from the metropolitan centers. With great rapidity one improvement followed another and as the radio became more dependable its popularity increased. Battery troubles were eliminated and the cost of operation was cut down by the construction of sets that derive their power entirely from the lighting circuit in the home. The controls were so simplified that they could be operated by a child. Improvements in loud speakers made possible a more accurate reproduction of the original programs. By means of telephone lines radio studios were extended to outside places such as concert halls and athletic fields, thus making it possible to transmit programs publicly given and report athletic contests play-by-play by announcers actually on the field. By a more elaborate use of this same method different

[12] Dun's Review, October 31, 1931, p. 8.

broadcasting stations were connected and there were built up national networks that broadcast programs from a common center with practically no limitations because of distance. In 1931 one hundred and fifty stations located in large cities in all sections of the country utilized programs sponsored by the National Broadcasting Company and the Columbia Broadcasting System.[13] Under the auspices of these nation-wide chains musicians and entertainers of wide repute appear on the programs and important games and contests are broadcast to the entire country.

So effectively organized is the system of radio broadcasting that the purchaser of a radio set is given the assurance that he has thereby gained access to the vast theater of the air with its almost unlimited facilities for entertainment. He expects with no further cost to himself than the expense of operation and upkeep to be able to tune in at any hour of the day or evening on a varied assortment of programs sufficiently diversified to provide the kind of entertainment desired. This has been made possible in this country by utilizing radio broadcasting for advertising purposes. Programs are sponsored by advertisers who thereby secure publicity for their wares and gain goodwill because of the free entertainment provided. Since the revenue derived from advertisers depends upon the size of the radio audience, the tendency is to present a popular program designed to please the largest number of people. This tendency is accentuated through the competition between rival radio stations, each seeking the largest possible audience in order to strengthen its position as an advertising medium. Meanwhile, the advertisers who sponsor the programs are no longer content merely to have their names mentioned at the beginning and end of their broadcast. Announcers must take time between musical numbers to describe the excellence of the commodities being advertised, and it is becoming customary for a leading member of the firm to appear before the microphone and deliver his per-

[13] President's Research Committee on Social Trends, *Recent Social Trends in the United States*, Chapter IV.

sonal message to the people. A recent survey showed that on the average 5.6 per cent of the time on the air is devoted to station announcements, 20.9 per cent to the advertising message, and 73.5 per cent to entertainment.[14] This growing emphasis upon advertising is undoubtedly making radio entertainment less attractive to the public and may eventually lead to less enthusiastic and diminishing audiences.

Whatever may be the shortcomings growing out of the commercialization of radio broadcasting, there has been no strong movement in this country in the direction of government operation and control as is the general practice abroad. The Federal Radio Commission appointed in 1927 has through its control over wave lengths prevented undue multiplication of broadcasting stations but exercises no supervision over the radio programs. Many believe that the competitive conditions under which radio has developed in this country have stimulated new improvements and keep the broadcasting stations on the lookout for novel features of compelling interest. A great deal of the criticism of the commercial control of radio comes from those who would prefer a larger use of the radio for purposes of education and cultural improvement. Its development in America has been primarily as a means of entertainment and in this field it has gained wide public favor. The public turns to the radio for its dance music, humorous dialogues, bedtime stories, light opera, and vivid portrayal of baseball and football games, prize fights, and other contests important in the world of sport. Its successful provision of entertainment of this kind has made possible the spectacular growth of radio during the past decade and if the promise of television can be fulfilled, as now seems probable, it will likely become even more securely entrenched in public favor.

[14] New York *Times*, January 24, 1932, p. 14.

CHAPTER VII

SOCIAL ORGANIZATION IN THE FIELD OF LEISURE

THE modern trend toward organization, which has penetrated every phase of American life, is especially notable in the field of recreation and leisure time. In order to meet the growing demand for enjoyable ways of spending leisure, corporate action has become as necessary as in other fields of human activity. Increasing leisure and higher standards of living have brought within reach of the mass of the people enlarged opportunities for recreation, far too great to be utilized by individual initiative alone. The machinery of government, philanthropic societies, business organizations, and cooperative associations of many kinds have been called upon in the building of the modern recreational world. This trend toward the organization of leisure has been accentuated by an increasing insistence upon a large variety of leisure-time activities available wherever needed, varying with the seasons, and adapted to the requirements of all classes and conditions of people. The supplanting of the more simple pleasures of an earlier day by games and sports and social activities of a more elaborate nature requiring expensive facilities for their enjoyment has ushered in a regime of clubs and associations that have become a characteristic feature of modern recreation. The devotee of sport or the aspirant for social diversions attains his goal most readily by affiliation with organizations that specialize in activities of his choice. Little opportunity is left for those who prefer to develop their own recreational interests independently. All are engulfed in the growing multiplicity of organizations with their standardized programs and activities which now dominate the recreational life of the people.

Recreational Associations Not a New Development.—

The use of organization to facilitate recreation is of course nothing new. The coming together of formal and informal groups for the enjoyment of leisure goes back into the remote past and must not be thought of as a peculiarity of contemporary life. During the colonial days we read of the organization of literary societies where, after the literary program, refreshments were served and "if the meetings took place in almost any other place than the parsonage, the refreshments were followed by an hour of dancing."[1] In the eastern community discussed by J. M. Williams in *An American Town*, there was an athletic club as early as 1878, and ten years later there were five different clubs of this sort flourishing at the same time. In this same community a debating club was organized about 1850 and functioned until 1887. Various other miscellaneous clubs such as the Grange, dancing clubs, musical clubs, social clubs, card clubs, etc. are listed for the period from 1875 to 1900. In 1892, sixteen of these clubs were active. Very similar facts were reported by N. L. Sims in his study of a community in northeastern Indiana.[2] There were only nine years between 1869 and 1900 when there was not at least one athletic club, and in some years there were two, three, and even four clubs active at the same time. This community was close to a small lake which was the focus of a great deal of the recreational interest of the people. Twenty-six different lake clubs were organized between 1874 and 1910, one of which was in existence for the whole period, and in 1895 sixteen of them were in active operation. In this community there were also 22 different social clubs existing at one time or another between 1869 and 1910. The study of Middletown brought out the fact that there were 92 clubs in that city in 1890, a ratio of 125 people per club as compared with a ratio of 80 per club in 1924.[3] A description of

[1] Helen E. Smith, *Colonial Days and Ways*, The Century Co., 1900, p. 270.

[2] N. L. Sims, *A Hoosier Village*, pp. 114–119, Columbia University Studies in History, Economics and Public Law, Vol. 46, New York, 1912.

[3] Robert S. Lynd and Helen M. Lynd, *Middletown*, New York, 1929, pp. 285–286.

the situation in Clarke County, Ohio, written in 1900 states that "Even as late as twenty years ago, scarcely a rural community failed to have a large and flourishing literary society, debating club, or singing school . . . There were 98 fraternal bodies in Springfield in 1900 with a total membership of 11,311 . . . There are many club organizations among the women of Springfield. It is impossible to enumerate all the women's clubs of today,—their name is legion."[4]

Further evidence bearing on this point is the fact that some of the most important leisure-time associations of the present day originated prior to 1900. Practically all of the large fraternal orders were well established by this date. The Young Men's and Young Women's Christian Associations and the Young Men's Hebrew Association were all organized before 1875. There were in 1888 athletic clubs of sufficient number and development to form the Amateur Athletic Union of the United States and by 1890 to change the Amateur Athletic Union from an association of athletic clubs to a federation of such associations. Social clubs, athletic clubs, dramatic clubs, etc. have had a long history as well as a most rapid, recent growth. There can be no doubt of the increasing role of organization in the field of leisure but this movement has its roots deep in the past. Associations of this kind have made their great advance during a period of extraordinary urban development and apparently have no more than kept pace with expansion in other fields of human activity.

Types of Leisure-time Associations.—Even a casual study of the field of leisure brings convincing proof of the multiplicity of organizations of widely different kinds which constitute in a very real sense the framework of the modern recreational world. Around these organizations revolve the innumerable activities which occupy man's attention during his hours of freedom from daily toil. The vast number of these associations has been made possible not merely by increasing leisure but by an expanding world of activity and freedom of movement with its varied oppor-

[4] E. S. Todd, *A Sociological Study of Clarke County, Ohio*, pp. 82–83.

tunities for enjoyment and its difficult problems awaiting solution. In addition to the diversions, sports, and amusements that occupy so many of the hours of leisure, a large amount of time is given to the promotion of causes, to efforts to improve social and civic conditions, and to the advancement of hobbies and special interests both of a personal and general nature. This tendency has made inevitable the growth of a wide network of organizations many of which are of such serious purpose and seem so closely related to the struggle for existence that their role in the recreational world is not readily apparent. When we add to organizations of this general type those that deal more directly with recreational interests, we are confronted by a confusing array of clubs, associations, societies, and organizations of widely divergent types that do not readily · fall into any orderly classification.

Examples of some of the more common types of leisure-time associations are fraternal orders; insurance societies of the fraternal type; college fraternities and sororities; propagandist societies; learned societies; business associations such as chambers of commerce; civic and social improvement societies; ethical and religious organizations; associations of military veterans; patriotic societies; associations on the order of the Klu Klux Klan; immigrant and racial societies; ancestral societies; luncheon clubs; motor clubs; trade unions and labor organizations; city clubs maintaining club buildings in downtown areas; country, hunting, fishing, yacht, and similar clubs; golf, tennis, baseball, and other athletic clubs; music, art, drama, and book clubs; nature and outdoor clubs; social and bridge clubs; political clubs; professional athletic clubs; federations of women's clubs; and many others that might be included. For the purposes of this chapter these organizations have been roughly divided into three general classes: (1) those that utilize leisure for the attainment of serious ends; (2) those that fall within the field of sports, games, and amusements; and (3) those concerned with the promotion of public recreational activities. Satisfactory statistical data

[125]

showing the growth and present status of associations are difficult to obtain and in many cases do not exist. For this reason as well as because of limitations of space, no attempt will be made to discuss in detail all the organizations listed above. Conclusions concerning trends must be based on such general facts as are available together with a more detailed study of certain types of associations that seem to be fairly representative of the whole field of leisure-time organization.

Quasi-recreational Associations.—Under this heading are included the varied types of associations that attempt to organize leisure for a serious purpose rather than directly in the interests of recreation. Their chief characteristic is the promotion of a cause or the attainment of a desired goal but their activities are carried on during the leisure time of their members and their program ordinarily includes some social or recreational features. Organizations of this kind cover a wide range of interests and may have little in common except their important role in the field of leisure time. Familiar examples of such associations are fraternal orders, luncheon clubs, propagandist societies, parent-teacher associations, and improvement clubs of different kinds. The establishment of organizations of this type comes about usually in response to specific needs, and their life cycle is of varying length depending upon their capacity to adjust their programs to changing conditions.

Among organizations in this wide field fraternal orders and secret societies stand out prominently because of their long history and large membership. The development of secret societies or lodges in this country, so far as this is measured by the organization of new societies, was primarily a movement of the last century (Table 36). Practically all of the important fraternal orders of the present day had their origin before 1900. Historically, they have been divided into five classes; Masonic organizations, patriotic societies, friendly societies, temperance societies, and insurance societies. The characteristic differences between these classes are disappearing, except that insurance societies are still to be distinguished from the others. Even here, however, this distinction is tending to disappear since many of the insurance societies have social members not participating in the insurance and some of the other societies have adopted certain insurance features.

TABLE 36.—DISTRIBUTION OF 191 FRATERNAL SOCIETIES, BY DATE OF ORGANIZATION[a]

Year	Number of societies organized	Year	Number of societies organized
1850–1859	1	1890–1899	73
1860–1869	6	1900–1909	29
1870–1879	26	1910–1919	13
1888–1889	39	1920–1929	4

[a] Listed in *Statistics of Fraternal Societies*, 1930.

Free masonry, which furnished the pattern for many of the leading fraternal orders, was introduced into the United States about 1730. By the year 1825 there was at least one Masonic lodge in every state then in the Union and the movement continued to spread as the population increased. During the last quarter of the nineteenth century there were organized several societies, the membership of which was limited to Masons or their near relatives, such societies as the Shriners, Eastern Star, Rosacruscians, etc. The modern patriotic societies began with the organization of the United American Mechanics in 1845, followed by the Sons of America in 1847, the Junior Order of United American Mechanics in 1853, Sons and Daughters of Liberty in 1875, and the Patriotic Order of Americans in 1897. The Independent Order of Odd Fellows, introduced from England in 1819, was the first of the friendly societies and was followed by the Ancient Order of Foresters in 1832. The first friendly society of American origin, the Improved Order of Red Men, was also established in the latter year. Among the other better known societies of this group are the Knights of Pythias (1864), the Benevolent and Protective Order of Elks (1866), and the Loyal Order of Moose (1888). Temper-

[127]

ance societies represent a special class of the friendly societies, the qualifications for membership including a pledge to
abstain from intoxicants. The Independent Order of
Rechabites was brought from England in 1842, in which
year was also organized the first American temperance
society, the Sons of Temperance. The Independent Order of
Good Templars, one of the largest of the present day societies of this kind, was organized in 1852. The insurance
societies, which now number approximately 200, had their
beginning in 1868 with the organization of the Ancient
Order of United Workmen. The societies of this kind gained
rapidly in popularity largely because of the widespread
prejudice that existed at that time against regular life insurance companies. Many difficulties were encountered in
putting the fraternal insurance business on a sound actu-
arial basis, but in spite of these financial problems the
insurance societies attracted a large following.

While the fraternal order movement has enjoyed widespread growth, having now an estimated membership of
35,000,000, available evidence seems to indicate that it is
near, if it has not already reached, the peak of its development. Masonic membership increased rather rapidly during
the early years of the twentieth century (Table 38) but
recently the rate of increase has declined to such an extent
that during the last two or three years membership gains
have been nearly offset by losses in membership. An analysis
of the regional distribution of gains and losses of this organization shows that with the exception of Iowa, Kansas, and
North Dakota, the only states showing losses in membership were located in the southern section of the country.
The lodges of the insurance societies reached their greatest
number in 1925 and since then have shown a marked decline. Their membership nearly doubled between 1905 and
1920 and continued to increase through 1929 but declined
about seven per cent the following year. Their recent slow
rate of growth is indicated by the fact that the membership
in 1930 was only slightly larger than in 1920 (Table 37). A
study of the membership of nine other leading fraternal

organizations not primarily insurance societies shows that their membership doubled between 1905 and 1925 but declined during the next five year period. In 1930 their

TABLE 37.—NUMBER OF MEMBERS AND NUMBER OF LODGES OF FRATERNAL INSURANCE SOCIETIES, 1905–1930[a]

Year	Members		Lodges	
	Number of members	Index number (1905 = 100)	Number of lodges	Index number (1905 = 100)
1905..................	5,111,480	100.0	87,758	100.0
1910..................	7,037,432	137.7	107,025	122.0
1915..................	8,436,768	165.1	121,390	138.3
1920..................	9,951,331	194.7	123,431	140.6
1925..................	10,765,680	210.6	127,835	145.7
1929..................	10,895,529	213.2	123,434	140.7
1930..................	10,123,669	198.1	120,789	137.6

[a] Compiled from *Statistics of Fraternal Societies*.

membership increased nine per cent but was still 500,000 less than in 1925 (Table 38).

TABLE 38.—MEMBERSHIP OF FRATERNAL SOCIETIES, 1905–1930[a]

Year	Masons[b] (in thousands)	Other non-insurance societies[c] (in thousands)	Insurance societies[d] (in thousands)
1905.......................	989	3,696	5,111
1910.......................	1,310	4,823	7,037
1915.......................	1,671	5,468	8,437
1920.......................	2,057	6,640	9,951
1925.......................	3,174	7,463	10,766
1929.......................	3,484	6,390	10,896
1930.......................	3,505	6,966	10,124

[a] Compiled from *Statistics of Fraternal Societies*. (Not all Fraternal Societies are included in this table.)

[b] Includes membership in the United States and Canada.

[c] Data for the entire period were available only for the following societies: Independent Order of Odd Fellows; Independent Order of Rechabites; Benevolent and Protective Order of Elks; Knights of Pythias; Independent Order of Good Templars; Fraternal Order of Eagles; Improved Order of Red Men; Foresters of America; and Junior Order United American Mechanics.

[d] Includes all such societies reporting in the years indicated.

This slowing up in membership has been accompanied by a declining attendance at lodge meetings and less interest in their rites and ceremonies. The recreational features of the lodge have been pushed into the background by the automobile, the radio, the moving picture, and other modern opportunities for the enjoyment of leisure. People have become much less dependent upon its gatherings for their social occasions. The fraternal orders that carry insurance benefits are finding it more difficult to compete with the regular insurance companies. Since 1910 the amount of annual insurance written by fraternal societies has fallen from about one-third of the national total to less than one-fifteenth.[5] In spite of its decline, however, the fraternal order movement still possesses much of its former prestige. In many communities business and professional men find it to their interest to maintain their lodge connections, and many members of the working classes continue to look to these societies for their sickness and death benefits. The annual conventions of some of the societies attract thousands and must be ranked among the great gatherings of the present day. Even if the recent downward trend continues, as now seems probable, fraternal orders have such a large following that they will likely occupy for years a prominent place among leisure-time associations.

TABLE 39.—NUMBER OF COLLEGE FRATERNITIES AND SORORITIES AND NUMBER OF CHAPTERS, 1883–1929[a]

Year	Fraternities		Sororities	
	Number of fraternities	Number of chapters	Number of sororities	Number of chapters
1883...............	26	484	6	44
1898...............	29	785	8	89
1912...............	41	1,212	17	352
1920...............	51	1,602	19	572
1927...............	74	2,430	29	999
1929...............	82	5,910	35	1,251

^a Compiled from Baird's *Manual of American College Fraternities.*

The college Greek letter societies, which may be regarded as a part of the secret society movement although they have

[5] Article on "Fraternal Orders," *Encyclopaedia of the Social Sciences*, Vol. 6: 425.

developed independently, have shown a marked upward trend during recent years. Phi Beta Kappa, organized in 1776, was the first of these societies and the only one for nearly fifty years. Acording to Baird's *Manual of American College Fraternities*, 26 college fraternities were organized prior to 1870 and then followed a period of 18 years without the formation of another new Greek letter society. Their period of most rapid growth has been between 1920 and 1929 when the number of national college fraternities increased from 51 to 82 and their chapters from 1,602 to 5,910. During this same period the college sororities grew from 19 to 35 and their chapters from 572 to 1,251 (Table 39). This remarkable expansion of college secret societies has been made possible by the great increase in the number of college students as well as by the more favorable attitude toward such organizations by college administrative authorities. These Greek letter societies have become widely popular and generally dominate the social life of the higher educational institutions.

Another recently developed type of leisure-time association is the luncheon club, which has had a phenomenal growth throughout the entire country. The movement to build up formal clubs of this kind with a standardized procedure originated in Chicago with the organization of the first Rotary club in 1905. The second club of this type was not organized until three years later. By the year 1910 there were 16 Rotary clubs which then formed a national association now known as the Rotary International. The first Kiwanis club was organized in Detroit in 1915 and the national federation called the Kiwanis International was formed a year later. The Lions International was established in 1917 by the affiliation of a number of independent luncheon clubs, the name of Lions being taken from a group of clubs organized in the southwest.

While these three federations are most widely known, the movement has spread until there are now 27 different national organizations of luncheon clubs. The extraordinary growth of this movement, judged by the increase in the number of member clubs of the various federations, has occurred during the past decade (Table 40). Between 1920 and 1929 the local Rotary clubs quadrupled, the

TABLE 40.—NUMBER OF CLUBS AND MEMBERSHIP OF ROTARY INTERNATIONAL KIWANIS INTERNATIONAL, AND LIONS INTERNATIONAL, 1917–1931[a]

Year	Rotary		Kiwanis		Lions	
	Number of clubs	Member-ship	Number of clubs	Member-ship	Number of clubs	Member-ship
1917	311	32,000	52	5,900	25	800
1919	530	45,000	138	15,500	42	2,364
1921	975	70,000	538	47,970	245	13,739
1923	1,493	89,700	1,043	78,961	640	32,477
1925	2,096	108,000	1,382	94,422	939	43,647
1927	2,627	129,000	1,638	100,849	1,183	52,965
1929	3,178	144,000	1,812	103,308	1,849	69,778
1931	3,460	157,000	1,879	87,951	2,491	80,456

[a] Compiled from data furnished by the national headquarters of these clubs. The figures include clubs outside as well as inside the United States.

Kiwanis clubs increased seven times, and the Lions clubs sixteen times. In 1932 Rotary had 2,443 clubs in the United States with 107,385; Kiwanis, 1,873 clubs with 77,910 members; and Lions, 2,580 clubs with 76,750 members. Most of the other organizations are small, Optimist International, for example, having only 121 clubs. The three largest federations mentioned above had in the United States in 1932 some 6,900 clubs with approximately 262,000 members. The total membership of all luncheon clubs in the 27 federations was estimated in 1932 to be more than 500,000.[6]

Luncheon clubs at first were found only in large cities. Every city of more than 500,000 population had a Rotary club by 1912. There were only six cities of more than 100,-000 population that did not have Rotary clubs by 1915 and all of these had such clubs by 1922. As luncheon clubs became more popular, the movement began to spread to the smaller cities and towns. A study of a random sample

[6] Estimate based on data supplied by the national headquarters of the larger federations.

of 490 Rotary clubs showed that only one per cent of the clubs organized between 1915 and 1919 were in towns under 2,500, whereas 54 per cent of those organized between 1925 and 1929 were in towns of this class. Apparently the Kiwanis and Lions clubs have been moving in the same direction although not so rapidly. Since these three older federations already dominate the small town field, it is not likely that many clubs affiliated with the other federations will be able to find a foothold in these smaller places.

The luncheon club movement gained its first strength in the East North Central states and then expanded southward through the Mississippi Valley. At the present time luncheon clubs are fairly uniformly distributed throughout the entire country but certain regional differences are still apparent (Table 41). There are not as many Kiwanis

TABLE 41.—PER CENT DISTRIBUTION OF LUNCHEON CLUBS IN RELATION TO POPULATION, BY GEOGRAPHICAL DIVISIONS[a]

Geographical division	Popu-lation, 1930	Per cent distribution of								
		Rotary clubs[b]	Kiwanis clubs	Lions clubs	Opti-mist clubs	Y's men's clubs	Round table clubs	A B C clubs	Gyro clubs	Civi-tan clubs
United States........	100.0	100.0	100.0	100.0	100.0	100.0	100.0	100.0	100.0	100.0
New England........	6.7	8.0	4.8	5.3	0.8	17.7	4.5	.....	.....	6.0
Middle Atlantic......	21.4	15.1	13.4	10.7	16.9	21.0	10.6	25.8	9.5	3.4
East North Central...	20.6	20.2	23.0	15.6	28.4	31.9	19.7	27.4	38.1	11.4
West North Central..	10.8	14.1	11.5	18.1	10.0	10.9	4.5	3.3	16.6	4.0
South Atlantic.......	12.9	13.5	16.1	8.7	4.6	4.2	7.6	17.7	2.4	39.6
East South Central...	8.0	6.7	6.4	5.3	7.7	3.4	3.0	9.7	.....	25.5
West South Central..	9.9	10.4	8.0	18.3	8.5	5.9	13.7	14.5	.....	5.4
Mountain...........	3.0	5.1	5.1	8.5	3.1	0.8	6.1	1.6	4.8	1.3
Pacific.............	6.7	6.9	11.7	9.5	20.0	4.2	30.3	.....	28.6	3.4

[a] Compiled from data supplied by the officials of the luncheon clubs.
[b] A random sample of 490 clubs.

and Lions clubs in New England and there are more in the Far West than would be expected when considered from the point of view of their proportion of the total urban population. There is also a marked concentration of Lions clubs in the West South Central states. Nearly all the smaller

[133]

federations show distinct regional concentrations. Taking all the organizations together, the luncheon club movement has had its greatest development on the Pacific coast and has made its least advance in New England. In the other regions the per cent distribution of clubs is approximately the same as the per cent distribution of the population.

The trend of growth of luncheon clubs is still mounting upward but the slightly smaller membership increases during recent years indicates that the movement may not greatly expand in the future.[7] Further rapid gains in membership, especially of the older federations, seem extremely improbable when we consider that the membership is highly selective and that the most available field is already well covered. It is significant that luncheon clubs, whose membership has been limited almost entirely to business and professional men, have shown no tendency to expand by opening their doors to the general public. Neither have they set a pattern for the organization of similar clubs among other classes of the population. They originated among the more successful urban leaders and still remain a leisure-time association for this class.

Whether these clubs will prove to be anything more than a passing fad, it is difficult to forecast. Undoubtedly the weekly use of the lunch hour for the promotion of good fellowship is a device well suited to those whose daily work is carried on in the heart of the city. Their distinctive rites and ceremonies, their civic welfare enterprises, and their strong overhead organization with its publications and promotive activities serve to keep up the morale of the local clubs and tend to give the movement a greater degree of permanence.

These examples of associations that combine recreational features with the promotion of serious objectives are representative of an expanding group of organizations that invade every field of activity and command wide public support. Because of the increasing demand of the public

[7] The number of Kiwanis Clubs has been practically stationary since 1930, with a decline of 14 per cent in membership between 1930 and 1932.

for recreation, these organizations are more and more modifying their original programs to make room for entertainment as well as for serious work. This tendency is especially notable in the activities of civic clubs, trade unions, business associations, religious organizations, and other groups organized for a serious purpose. The need for relaxation perhaps is no more keenly felt than in the past, but the giving of some time and attention to entertainment and diversion is now accepted as a matter of course and no apologies are made for it. An excellent illustration of this trend is the modern convention now so widely popular, where the amusement and recreational activities are in many instances given a prominent place on the program and constitute for many of the delegates the chief attraction of the annual gathering. This tendency to mingle pleasure with work, to make room for the lighter side of life in the midst of serious undertakings, is a recent development, the importance of which can hardly be overestimated.

Recreational Clubs and Associations.—While organizations not directly concerned with recreation have become an important channel through which modern recreational needs are met, recent years have seen a remarkable growth of organizations concerned solely with leisure-time diversions and amusements. The various games and sports that have risen to public favor. during the past generation are responsible for the establishment of many kinds of clubs and associations which bring together those desiring to participate in the same sport and enable them through corporate action to provide the necessary playing facilities. Examples of these are country clubs, golf clubs, fishing clubs, hunting clubs, tennis clubs, yacht clubs, and many others covering the wide range of modern sports. Since these clubs are privately maintained and in many cases are not directly affiliated with a national organization, it has not been possible to ascertain their present total number or their rate of increase over a period of years. For our most satisfactory, although incomplete, measure of the expansion

[135]

of these clubs, we must rely upon the records of taxes paid by such organizations to the federal government. In 1920, when a federal tax of 10 per cent was assessed on all dues of more than $10 a year, the amount received from this source was $5,198,001. Eight years later the federal tax receipts had almost doubled, the exact amount being $10,352,989. Beginning with the year 1929, through a modification of the federal law, clubs having annual dues of less than $25 were not required to pay taxes. In spite of this change in the basis of taxation, which exempted many small clubs that had previously come under the law, the tax receipts continued to increase during 1929 and 1930, and the amount paid by these organizations in 1930 amounted to $12,521,091. The following year, however, there was a decline of 8.3 per cent in the taxes collected from this source, a falling off due probably to the financial depression (Table 42). Even when ample allowance is made

TABLE 42.—RECEIPTS FROM TAXES ON THE DUES OF SOCIAL AND ATHLETIC CLUBS[a]

Year	Tax receipts	Year	Tax receipts
1920.	$5,198,001	1926.	$10,073,838
1921.	6,159,817	1927.	10,436,020
1922.	6,615,633	1928.	10,352,989
1923.	7,170,730	1929.	11,245,254
1924.	8,009,861	1930.	12,521,091
1925.	8,690,588	1931.	11,477,723

[a] Compiled from the Annual Reports of the United States Commissioner of Internal Revenue. A 10 per cent tax was levied on annual dues in excess of $10 from 1921 to 1928, and on annual dues in excess of $25 from 1929 to 1931.

for increases in annual dues, it is quite clear that this class of association has at least doubled in income if not in numbers during the past decade. The rise of golf and tennis clubs since 1900, which has already been discussed in an earlier chapter, furnishes further evidence on this point and helps to confirm the conclusion that the recent growth of clubs in the field of sports is unprecedented.

In addition to these local recreational clubs there have come into existence many organizations national in scope whose functions are to standardize rules and regulations, control conditions of competitive play, and conduct or authorize sectional and national tournaments and athletic meets. Among the more general organizations of this type that have wide jurisdiction over a large number of different sports, are the Amateur Athletic Union of the United States, National Amateur Athletic Federation, National Collegiate Athletic Association, Intercollegiate Association of Amateur Athletes of America, American Physical Education Association, and the American Olympic Association. Of great importance also are the national organizations established to promote the interests of a single sport, as for example, the Amateur Fencers League of America, National Association of Scientific Angling Clubs, National Archery Association, the American Bowling Congress, American Canoe Association, United States Golf Association, United States Field Hockey Association, United States Amateur Hockey League, National Horseshoe Pitchers Association, Amateur Skating Union of the United States, United States Intercollegiate Lacrosse Association, American Lawn Bowling Association, American Roque League, National Ski Association, United States Lawn Tennis Association, National Association of Amateur Oarsmen, Amateur Trapshooting Association, American Snowshoe Union, National Cycling Association, National Amateur Casting Association, and United States Football Association. Organizations of this kind furnish the machinery for orderly competition between different groups and safeguard the interests of the sport they sponsor. These associations, national in scope, are by no means a new device for some were established during the closing quarter of last century. They have, however, become more numerous during the past two decades and are supported by a much wider constituency than ever before.

Besides these organizations which are concerned primarily with athletic sports and outdoor games, there are in every community bridge clubs, dancing clubs, and other social clubs around which is organized a large share of the social life of the mass of the people. Associations and clubs of this kind may be very informal in nature and frequently lack continuity because of the mobility that is so characteristic of modern urban life. It is not possible to make even a rough estimate of the number of clubs of this kind since they are so ephemeral in nature but recent community studies bear ample witness of their wide vogue as well as their importance in present day recreation. The increase in the manufacture of playing cards has at least partially been stimulated by the recent widespread interest in bridge and gives some indication of the enlarged activities of bridge and other card clubs. Federal tax was paid in 1931 upon 49,329,-062 packs of playing cards. The production of playing cards increased nearly three times during the past 30 years and made a gain of 25 per cent between 1920 and 1930 (Table 43). The taboo against cards as well as against dancing,

TABLE 43.—NUMBER OF PACKS OF PLAYING CARDS ON WHICH FEDERAL TAX WAS PAID, 1900–1930[a]

Year	Number of packs	Index number (1900 = 100)
1900	16,550,533	100
1910	28,276,117	169
1920	38,605,775	231
1930	48,192,925	289

[a] Compiled from the Annual Reports of the United States Commissioner of Internal Revenue.

which formerly prevented many from participating in these diversions, is much less effective than formerly and in many communities has entirely disappeared. This more liberal attitude toward these amusements has not only greatly increased the spontaneous card playing and dancing at casual meetings of friends, but has given new impetus to the tendency of small, congenial groups to organize for the better enjoyment of these popular leisure-time activities. No form of leisure-time organization is more widespread than clubs of this type and all the available evidence points to their continuing popularity.

Organizations Promoting Public Recreation.—The American trend toward organization is also evident in the growth of agencies concerned with the development of wholesome recreation either as their major activity or as part of a broader social, intellectual, religious, or character building program. Representative of this type of organizations are social settlements, school community centers, community churches, youth service associations, and associations established primarily for the promotion of the public recreation movement.

In a very real sense interest in public recreation began with the establishment of social settlements in the congested districts of large cities during the last two decades of the nineteenth century. The settlement leaders from the start became interested in the recreational problems of their neighborhood and endeavored to meet them by building up the social settlement as a recreational center for the people living within reach of its influence. Under their auspices some of the first children's playgrounds were conducted and their leadership was prominent in the expansion of municipal recreation activities.

The social settlement movement gained considerable headway during the nineties and by the end of the second decade of the present century had spread into many of the large cities throughout the entire country. The recent progress of the settlement movement is difficult to measure because its work has become so closely allied with that of similar institutions that comparable lists of settlements over a period of years are not available. If we consider only the settlements that belong to the National Federation of Settlements, which by no means include all engaged in some form of settlement activities, the movement appears to be practically at a standstill as far as increase in numbers is concerned. The federation membership in 1919 numbered 156 and in 1930 it had increased to only 160.[8] Since the 1930 list includes 44 settlements which were not members

[8] *Proceedings* of the Ninth Conference of Settlements, 1919. *Neighborhood, A Settlement Quarterly,* December, 1930.

of the federation in 1919, at least 40 during this period must have dropped their membership in that organization and perhaps had discontinued their work. In 1930, as in 1919, ninety per cent of the settlements were located in cities of 100,000 or more, which indicates that the movement is still confined to large cities with no marked tendency to spread into smaller municipalities. During this period the settlements belonging to the national federation slightly declined in number in the northeastern and southern states and increased in the north central and Pacific coast states.

While the social settlements that fall strictly within this classification may not be increasing in numbers, they have set a pattern for neighborhood work and have stimulated the growth of closely related organizations in different fields of activity. Community field houses, community and institutional churches, parish houses, special industrial schools, and recreational centers under various auspices are largely outgrowths of the settlement movement and the success of these more specialized organizations has made less necessary the further expansion of the older institution. Nevertheless the social settlements continue to play a large part in the recreational life of large cities and those that have good facilities for sports and games have an especially large following.

Another type of organization that has done much to develop public recreation is the school community center. The first beginnings toward this so-called wider use of the public school plant go back to the first decade of the present century and were initiated by recreation leaders interested in using school playgrounds and school buildings after school hours for leisure-time activities. This community use of the public school was given great impetus during the World War through the efforts of the Council of National Defense to make the school the headquarters for the promotion of local war work. The most recent survey of school community centers in 1924 showed that there were at that time 1,569 centers located in 722 cities, villages, and townships. Between 1919 and 1924 the number of cities over

5,000 population having school centers increased from 107 to 240, a gain of 124 per cent.[9] In spite of this considerable progress, school centers in 1924, after 17 years of promotion, were being maintained in only 13 per cent of the cities over 5,000 and in only 4 per cent of all incorporated places. It is unfortunate that no figures are available showing the present number of school centers throughout the United States. Apparently the movement is making comparatively slow headway, partly because it has not been widely supported by the school authorities and more especially because of the increasing competition with other recreational opportunities of many kinds.

The administration and control of school community centers vary in different places. Originally they grew out of private initiative and effort and in many cases have been carried on under the auspices of a local community center association. The recent trend seems to be in the direction of official control, for 61 per cent of the school centers in 1924 were administered by school boards.[10] The activities sponsored by these centers have covered a wide field but the chief emphasis has usually been upon programs of a recreational nature. In 1924 athletics, which was reported by 70 per cent of the school centers studied, ranked as the most popular activity. The next most important use of the school building, reported by 50 per cent of the centers, was a meeting place for club groups of various kinds.[11] Since modern school plants are being more adequately equipped with facilities for games, athletic contests, dancing, and social gatherings, their use after school hours by the members of the community seems likely to become more widespread as the public recreation movement advances.

The school, of course, is only one of other possible centers of community life and it has been inevitable that

[9] E. T. Glueck, *The Community Use of Schools*, 1927, pp. 38–39, E. T. Glueck, *Extended Use of School Buildings*, U. S. Bureau of Education, Bulletin No. 5, 1927.
[10] E. T. Glueck, *The Community Use of Schools*, pp. 82–83.
[11] *Ibid.*, p. 113.

other efforts should be made to build up community recreation centers. In the downtown residential areas of large cities institutional churches, patterned somewhat after the social settlements, have enlarged their traditional functions by providing playgrounds, opening their rooms to neighborhood gatherings, and establishing social and recreational clubs for the people. More recently churches with this type of program are usually called community churches and have gained their greatest foothold in rural and small town communities. Of the 1,296 community churches reporting in 1927, 1,036 were located in towns under 2,500 population or in the open country.[12] Scarcely more than a hundred were located in cities of more than 25,000 population. During recent years an increasing number of churches have become interested in providing some form of recreation for their own members if not for the people living in their neighborhood. This movement has not, however, gone forward with great rapidity because of the still widely prevailing belief that the work of the church should be limited as far as possible to spiritual affairs.

Prominently identified with the development of recreational programs are the youth service associations which endeavor to promote the social and moral welfare of youth through activities that are largely recreational in nature. Of the fifteen leading national organizations of this type, five were established between 1851 and 1882 while the remainder are a product of the present century. The oldest group of associations, which are maintained primarily for young men and women, enjoyed a period of rapid expansion during the early part of this century and for the most part have shown a marked decline in their rate of growth during the decade following the World War. The Young Men's Christian Association has during recent years had a slow rate of membership growth and actually lost ground during 1930 (Table 44). The number of its local associa-

[12] F. Ernest Johnson, *The Social Work of the Churches*, Department of Research and Education of the Federal Council of Churches of Christ, 1930, p. 53.

tions, moreover, declined from 2,069 in 1920 to 1,435 in 1931.[13] The Young Women's Christian Association increased its local associations from 181 in 1915 to 441 in 1925 and since this latter date has gone forward much more slowly.[14] The membership of the Knights of Columbus reached a peak of 772,000 in 1923 and then declined to 637,000 in 1930. The Jewish organizations, on the other hand, have gained consistently during the past decade and still show a strong upward trend.[15]

The associations that are specially concerned with the development of programs for boys and girls are of more recent origin and on the whole are making much more rapid advance than the other youth service associations. The Girl Scouts increased their membership 356 per cent between 1920 and 1930 and the Camp Fire Girls made a gain of 117 per cent during this same period. The Boy Scouts, which were organized in this country in 1910, attained a membership of nearly 630,000 within 20 years but their rate of growth was much slower between 1925 and 1930 than during the first half of this decade (Table 44). The

TABLE 44.—MEMBERSHIP OF YOUNG MEN'S CHRISTIAN ASSOCIATION, BOY SCOUTS, GIRL SCOUTS, AND CAMP FIRE GIRLS, 1920–1930[a]

Year	Young Men's Christian Association	Boy Scouts	Girl Scouts	Camp Fire Girls
1920	821,756	389,352	62,248	96,756
1925	925,216	593,132	138,174	155,053
1929	1,086,862	606,396	239,519	201,239
1930	1,034,019	629,303	283,931	209,980

[a] Compiled from Yearbooks of the Young Men's Christian Association, Annual Reports of the Boy Scouts of America, and from data supplied by the national headquarters of the organizations.

remarkable expansion of organizations for boys and girls stands out as one of the notable advances in the field of

[13] Year Books of the Young Men's Christian Association.
[14] Data supplied by the National Board of the Young Women's Christian Association.
[15] President's Research Committee on Social Trends, *Recent Social Trends in the United States*, Chapter XX.

recreation. It is estimated that such associations enroll approximately 2,100,000 boys and 1,152,000 girls.[16]

The status of the youth service associations has been greatly strengthened by the increasing recognition of the necessity of providing more facilities for wholesome recreation for those living in crowded urban environments. The club buildings maintained by some of these organizations, their summer camps, their entertainment features, directed play activities, and recreational programs have become an important leisure-time resource for large numbers of people. The modern demand for more adequate club buildings and recreational equipment as well as for better trained personnel has brought about a rapid increase in the expenditures of these organizations which are dependent for a large measure of their support upon private philanthropy. While the youth service associations occupy a relatively less important position than was the case before the recent expansion of public recreational facilities, they are supported by a large and loyal constituency and are likely to continue to play an influential role for many years in the recreational world.

Besides the organizations already mentioned, there are many local associations whose sole function is the promotion of some phase of the movement for public recreation. Playground and recreation associations, community service leagues and boards, community house organizations, social center associations, and neighborhood leagues are examples of the type of local organizations that are now actively in work in cities and towns in all sections of the country. There were few organizations of this kind before 1900 and their period of most rapid development has been since the World War. It has been largely through their activities and influence that public opinion has been molded in favor of a wider expansion of public recreation facilities. National leadership in this field has been furnished by the National Recreation Association, which was established in 1906

[16] *Preliminary Committee Reports* of the White House Conference on Child Health and Protection, pp. 357, 360.

as the Playground Association of America. Its emphasis has been primarily upon the building up of public recreation under governmental auspices. Especially notable among its many activities are its promotion each year of a National Recreation Congress, its publication of an important monthly journal, one issue of which is a yearbook containing the best available statistical record of the progress of the public recreation movement, and its special field studies, as for example its recent reports on municipal and county parks. Through its publications, field studies, annual conferences, activities of field workers, and training of recreation leaders, it has become the guiding force in the field of public recreation.

Summary of Recent Trends.—The extraordinary emphasis upon organizations during and immediately following the World War is apparently giving way to a more rational appraisal of their value. As associations have become more numerous, the mere fact of belonging to them gives less prestige to individual members. People are therefore less inclined to join an organization simply because it seems to be the thing to do. The vogue of the "joiner" is on the decline. Organization is accepted as a necessary device for accomplishing desired ends and is valued only so far as it is suited for this purpose. This more selective and critical attitude toward recreational clubs and associations tends to give them greater impermanence. Many run quickly through their life cycle and then give way to others. This is especially true of the almost unnumerable social clubs which come and go as recreational interests and fashions change from year to year.

Another trend is the greater emphasis upon recreational associations. Whereas institutions and organizations of a more general nature and with widely different functions were formerly one of the most important channels through which recreational needs were met, there has been within recent years a remarkable growth of associations and clubs specializing entirely in some phase of amusement and recreation. No longer is any camouflage necessary for those who are interested in play. Their purpose is now approached more directly and with more efficient results. Moreover, the kind of recreational organization that seems to prosper most is one that is highly specialized, catering to a group interested in a single sport or a limited number of sports that fit in well together. People are not inclined to band themselves together for purposes of general recreation. They join a golf club, a tennis club, or a bridge club, and secure the desired diversity of sports and amusements by belonging to the various organizations that provide the facilities they desire to secure. This specialized form of recreational clubs brings together congenial groups and facilitates the development of sport but it is an important factor in the mounting costs of recreation.

A final trend that may be mentioned is the expanding role of national associations which now occupy a position of dominance inconsistent with earlier traditions of local community control. Local clubs and associations with no national connections are far more rare than formerly and are generally regarded as possessing an unfortunate handicap which decreases their prestige and usefulness. Standardized patterns created by national associations and slavishly copied by their local representatives are becoming more and more the vogue. While this places limitations on local initiative, it promotes orderliness and uniformity which appear specially desirable in a world of increasing complexity. Whether it is luncheon clubs, fraternal societies, athletic associations, or character building organizations, each group quickly falls into its own national groove and rarely attempts to deviate from the pattern set up for it. This is by no means a new characteristic but it is a type of procedure that is becoming more and more widespread.

CHAPTER VIII

THE URBANIZATION OF RURAL RECREATION[1]

THE recreational trends discussed in the preceding chapters apply more particularly to the urban situation where the conditions of life have been most favorable for the development of leisure time activities and programs. In recreation as in other phases of community life, the city has set the patterns which gradually become diffused throughout the entire country. Recently this process of diffusion has been greatly accelerated by the unprecedented improvements in communication and transportation. As the barriers between city and country have broken down, the lure of urban sports and amusements has spread into the most sparsely settled and remote districts. One of the interesting transitions now taking place in rural communities is the decline of the traditional ways of spending leisure and the taking over of modern forms of recreation adapted from urban patterns. In this chapter an attempt is made to point out some of the important changes taking place in rural recreation and to determine, if possible, the extent of urbanization in this field of rural life.

Conditions of Rural Life Affecting Recreation.—Certain conditions peculiar to rural life, and to farming as an industry, have to a considerable degree been determining influences in the development of the recreational habits of the rural population. So long as these conditions continue, rural recreation will have features distinguishing it from urban recreation. But many of these conditions are being modified, or their influence minimized by other changes.

Isolation constitutes one of the most important factors incident to rural life (Table 45). In 1930 the farm population

[1] This chapter was prepared by E. W. Montgomery, assistant professor of sociology at the University of Kentucky.

[147]

AMERICANS AT PLAY

TABLE 45.—DISTRIBUTION OF FARMS BY TYPE OF ROAD ON WHICH LOCATED

Kind of road	Number of farms[a]	Per cent distribu- tion	Kind of road	Number of farms[a]	Per cent distribu- tion
Total...............	6,288,648	100.0	Gravel...............:	1,279,113	20.3
			Sand-clay.............	156,531	2.5
Concrete.............	202,594	3.2	Improved dirt..........	1,638,954	26.1
Brick................	13,180	0.2	Unimproved dirt........	2,279,989	36.3
Asphalt..............	72,011	1.1	All other (including not		
Macadam.............	306,397	4.9	reported..............	339,879	5.4

[a] U. S. Bureau of the Census, 15th Census, Agriculture, Vol. 2, pt. 1, p. 12.

had a density of about 20 persons per square mile of farm land.[2] This compares with a density of something over 7,000 per square mile in the larger cities.[3] The primary conse- quence of this isolation has been to make propinquity, rather than age, sex, or common interest, the basis for recreational association. There has been little change in the density of the rural population during the past half century, but improvements in the means of transportation have greatly reduced the importance of isolation as a feature of rural life. The number of automobiles on American farms increased by 93 per cent between 1920 and 1930, and in the latter year more than 90 per cent of the farms in Iowa and Nebraska, and more than 80 per cent of the farms in five other states had automobiles;[4] and with the increase in the number of automobiles have come improvements in the quality of roads. Testimony is general that as the means of transportation have improved, association on the basis of the neighborhood has slowly but surely declined.[5]

[2] U. S. Bureau of the Census, 15th Census, Population, Vol. 3, pt. 1, p. 30; Agriculture, Vol. 1, p. 8.

[3] U. S. Bureau of the Census, *Financial Statistics of Cities*, 1927, p. 86.

[4] U. S. Bureau of the Census, 15th Census, Agriculture, Vol. 2, pt. 1, pp. 12, 54.

[5] W. H. Baumgartel, *A Social Study of Ravalli County, Montana*, University of Montana, Agricultural Experiment Station, Bulletin No. 160, Bozeman, 1923; p. 21. L. F. Jackson, *The Play Party in Ripley County, Indiana*, Unpublished thesis, University of Chicago Library, 1915, pp. 11–12. J. H. Kolb, *Rural Pri- mary Groups*, University of Wisconsin, Agricultural Experiment Station, Re- search Bulletin No. 51, Madison, 1921, pp. 28, 32. J. H. Kolb and A. F. Wileden, *Special Interest Groups in Rural Society*, University of Wisconsin, Agricultural Experiment Station, Research Bulletin No. 84, Madison, 1927, p. 3. J. M. Williams, *An American Town*, New York, 1906, pp. 72–74.

The hours of labor on the farm constitute a second factor influencing rural recreation. The average farmer works from 10 to 12 hours per day, his wife almost as long, as also do his children, as they begin to assume responsibilities comparatively early in life.[6] Excessively long hours restrict the amount of time available for recreation, and leave the farmer and his family too fatigued at the end of the day to have much interest in any further activity. The most important change in farm life affecting this problem has been the introduction of labor saving machinery.

In considering the influence of the introduction of machinery on the availability of leisure, it must be remembered that farm work is by no means completely mechanized. There are many laborious forms of farm work for which machinery has not yet been devised; and furthermore, the cost of certain types of machinery is prohibitive except for large-scale production, whereas the majority of farms are comparatively small. In spite of phenomenal increases during the past decade, only 13 per cent of the farms had trucks and only 14 per cent had tractors in 1930 (Table 46).

TABLE 46.—MACHINERY AND OTHER FACILITIES ON FARMS AND NUMBER OF FARMS REPORTING, 1920, 1930[a]

Item	Number			Number of farms reporting		
	1920	1930	Per cent of increase	1920	1930	Per cent of increase
Motor trucks......................	139,169	900,385	547.0	131,551	845,335	542.6
Tractors.........................	246,083	920,021	273.9	229,332	851,457	271.3
Electric motors for farm work.......	(b)	386,191	.....	(b)	256,663	.....
Stationary gas engines..............	(b)	1,131,108	.....	(b)	945,000	.....
Water piped into dwelling...........	....	....	.....	643,899	994,202	54.4
Water piped into bathroom.........	....	....	.....	(b)	531,248	.....
Dwelling lighted by electricity......	....	....	.....	452,620	841,310[c]	85.9

[a] Adapted from U. S. Bureau of the Census, 15th Census, Agriculture, Vol. 2, pt. 1, p. 12.
[b] Not reported.
[c] Gas or electricity.

[6] J. O. Rankin, *The Use of Time in Farm Homes*, University of Nebraska, Agricultural Experiment Station, Bulletin No. 230, Lincoln, 1928, pp. 5, 28. R. L. Gillett, *A Study of Farm Labor in Seneca County, New York*, New York State Department of Farms and Markets, Bulletin No. 164, April 1924, p. 30.

It is also to be seriously questioned, particularly in the case of men, whether the introduction of machinery has resulted in a shorter working day. It is much more likely that the labor saved has been applied to the cultivation of larger areas of land or that machinery has been substituted for hired labor.[7] While labor saving machinery is probably not being used in the farm home as extensively as on the farm, its use has probably resulted more frequently in shorter hours; for the home-maker cannot undertake more home-making as her efficiency improves in the same way that the farm operator can undertake the cultivation of more land. It seems likely that the primary recreational significance of the introduction of machinery has been and will be in reducing fatigue, thereby freeing energy rather than time for recreational activities. While concrete data on this point are not available, such a conclusion seems justified in the absence of evidence to the contrary.

A third characteristic of rural life of recreational significance is the economic system in which production for consumption is an important element. Since from one-third to one-half of the farmer's living consists of goods produced on or contributed by the farm,[8] the amount of money passing through the farmer's hands is very small in relation to his total income in terms of commodities. A comparatively large proportion of this cash fund must go for those necessities that cannot be produced on the farm, leaving a minimum for recreational expenditures. This situation is reflected in the fact that recreation expenditures constitute only 1.4 per cent of the farmer's total cost of living, including his produce from the farm.[9] It is also reflected in the tardy development of commercial recreation in rural communities, and in the prevalence of amusements requiring little or no expensive equipment. The trend is very definitely toward production for exchange, the farmer devoting his labor more and more to exclusively agricultural produc-

[7] C. W. Gilbert, *An Economic Study of Tractors on New York Farms*, Cornell University, Agricultural Experiment Station, Bulletin No. 506, Ithaca, 1930, pp. 56, 61, 68.

[8] E. L. Kirkpatrick, *The Farmer's Standard of Living*, Century Co., 1929, p. 53.

[9] *Ibid.*, pp. 46, 183.

tion and accordingly purchasing an increasing variety of goods formerly produced on the farm. As the farmer's cash income increases with this trend toward production for the market, it may be anticipated that expenditures for recreation will bulk larger in his total expenditures.

Recreational Functions of Rural Institutions.—The absence of specialization is a characteristic of every phase of rural life. In the field of recreation this is manifested by the comparative lack of special facilities for recreational activities. In the absence of specialized recreational facilities, those functions have been assumed by, or become attached to, institutions and organizations established primarily for other purposes.

This combination of recreation with other activities appeared very early in the economic life of the rural community. Because of the absence of a laboring class and because of the system of production for consumption which provided little money with which labor could be hired, the American farmer developed a co-operative system of "trading help." Occasions for association were so infrequent in the early rural community and distances so great, that any circumstance that brought people together was likely to be valued as a recreational opportunity. These gatherings for co-operative labor, therefore, were also occasions for a large amount of spontaneous and informal visiting, good-natured chaffing and repartee, rough-and-tumble play among the young people, dancing and play-party games, and other recreational activities, to say nothing of the abundance of food that was invariably provided and the consumption of which was of such a character as to make it recreational. This association of work and play became so well established that each form of co-operative labor had its name, and the name applied to the particular form of labor came to designate primarily a recreational event: log-rollings, house- and barn-raisings, candle-dippings, sheep-shearings, carding-bees, spinning parties, corn-huskings or husking-bees, apple-corings, bean-hullings, sugar-boilings, wood-cuttings, quilting-bees.

These types of recreation have disappeared except in the marginal areas—those sections which, for one reason or another, have been isolated from the general progress of more fortunately situated communities. The disappearance of these types of recreation is associated primarily with changes in agricultural economy. Goods formerly produced on the farm or in the farm home for the use of the family, and the production of which was the occasion for neighborhood recreation, are now purchased. Furthermore, as production for exchange has increased, the farmer has more money with which to hire labor. Also, the substitution of machinery for labor has in many instances destroyed the necessity for co-operative labor, as has also the trend toward specialized farming.

The family unit, because of a combination of circumstances, is of considerably more importance in the rural community than in the urban community. The custom of open country settlement has limited continuous social contact to members of the same household, the nearest neighboring household being on the average a half-mile distant.[10] Family solidarity, originating in this isolation, was reinforced by the economic system in which the household was the unit of production, in contrast to urban economy in which industrial units are composed of individuals otherwise unrelated, and in which economic relations within the family are restricted to consumption.

The recreational significance of the unity of the rural family appears in several ways. An important proportion of all recreation is secured within the family group. The farm-child's play group is composed of his brothers and sisters, and the homestead constitutes his playground. The adult's evening hours of leisure are normally spent within the home and in association with other members of the same family. The family is also the typical unit of participation in recreational activities outside the home. Such events

[10] In 1930 the average farm consisted of 156.9 acres, making approximately four farms per square mile (U. S. Bureau of the Census, 15th Census, Agriculture, Vol. 1, p. 8).

are so infrequent that every member of the family wants to go to each one, and the use of a single conveyance is most convenient, if not always necessary. The home is also a recreational center for many events for which restaurants or other public rooms would be used in the city.

The conditions which made the family so important as a social unit are changing, however. While family units are just as far apart as ever, in fact a little farther apart,[11] the rapid development of transportation has rendered this spatial separation of secondary importance. The development of consolidated schools and the extension of the school terms are making play-groups composed of children of the same age and sex of relatively more importance than play groups composed of brothers and sisters. The extension of the school term is also a factor in that it makes the family less definitely a unit of economic production, since the child participates to a smaller extent in the farm work. As transportation has improved, the recreational facilities of nearby towns and cities have become more available, and amusements within the home have therefore become correspondingly less important. Clubs, particularly the extension clubs of the agricultural colleges, are coming into the communities and basing their programs on individual units rather than family units. All of these factors have weakened the recreational functions of the family.

The church has influenced rural recreation in two important ways: a considerable portion of the recreation of the rural community has been provided by the church and by its related organizations; and the church has exercised a restrictive influence over the recreation provided by other agencies in the community.

The church provided recreation for the members of the rural community in a variety of ways. The church services themselves may be viewed as recreational in part, in that they supplied opportunities for emotional expression, intel-

[11] The size of farms has gradually increased during the past fifty years. The average farm consisted of 133.7 acres in 1880; by 1930 the average farm had increased to 156.9 acres (U. S. Bureau of the Census, 14th Census, Vol. 5, p. 32; 15th Census, Agriculture, Vol. 2, pt. 1, p. 10).

lectual stimulation and participation in group activities, opportunities that are now supplied much more frequently by distinctly recreational organizations. Incidental to the religious services were the opportunities for visiting and the exchange of news before and after services, and, in the case of the camp meetings, the opportunities for games and other forms of amusement. Various organizations within the church also provided recreational events in the form of church suppers, Sunday school picnics, young people's parties, children's day and Easter "exercises," Christmas celebrations, etc.; and the regular meetings of these organizations also had certain recreational aspects.

Of equal importance was the role of the church in the censorship of amusements provided by other agencies. This censorship was made effective primarily through the church's part in the origin and maintenance of the mores by which individuals were made to feel the immorality of proscribed amusements. The prestige of the church and of the church group was such that few dared challenge the judgments about recreation for fear of the social ostracism so likely to follow. In a few communities the church was able to enforce its interdicts by some form of excommunication. Whatever its method, the church was able in most communities to outlaw in large measure such forbidden pleasures as dancing, card-playing, gambling, the theater, horse-racing, and pool and billiards, although the severity with which these bans were enforced varied with the particular amusements and with the community.

The recreational importance of the rural church has been weakened by a variety of changes in rural communities. First of all, the difficulties in transportation, which gave so much importance to all occasions of association, have been very largely overcome with the development of the automobile and improved roads. Furthermore, there have been developed many new sources and types of amusements which hold greater charm than those that were associated with the religious life of the community. The rural church itself in the opinion of many students is now in a period of decline. We find also that many of the amusements once so vigorously banned are now accepted by the church. It is possible, of course, that this represents the adaptation of the church to changing conditions and that the control of the church is only re-directed, but there is no evidence that the church is exercising control over recreation in any way comparable to the censorship that it once exercised.

The district school played an important part in recreation as long as rural social life was based upon associations within the neighborhood. It directly provided recreational opportunities in the spelling-bees, the various "exercises," the box-suppers and socials, and in the opportunities it afforded children to play together. In addition it was often used as an auditorium for activities unrelated to the school organization, such as lyceums, lectures, singing-schools, and dramatic performances.

In general it may be said that the rural school has lost its recreational functions entirely, or that these functions have been greatly modified by the patterns set by the urban schools. The role of the district school was due to the importance of the neighborhood in rural life and to the fact that the school was a neighborhood institution. As transportation facilities improved, as changes in agricultural economy destroyed the institution of co-operative labor, as differences in wealth and education encouraged social stratification, neighborhood association declined and with it the significance of the district school as a recreational institution.

The adaptation of the consolidated school to rural conditions has been of considerable importance in modifying the recreational role of the school. The bringing together of considerable numbers of children in the consolidated schools makes possible, as has been said, the formation of play-groups on the basis of similarity in sex and age and the adaptation of games to the interests and abilities of such specialized groups. It means also that group games involving larger numbers of children are possible. Furthermore, the consolidated school usually provides recreational equipment hitherto found only in the cities and the larger staff of teachers makes possible the supervision of recreational activities in a way previously unknown in the rural community.

Along with the consolidation of schools should be mentioned another movement of urban origin, the use of schools as community centers. This movement was developing in urban communities at just about the time that interest was being awakened in rural welfare. Rural leaders recognized in this type of organization an instrument readily adaptable to the needs and the traditions of the rural community, and efforts were made to foster the movement in rural communities. Available data indicate, however, that the movement is still essentially an urban movement. While 47 per cent of the places reporting the community use of schools[12] in 1924, for the survey sponsored by the United States Bureau of Education, were of less than 2,500 population,[13] it must be borne in mind that there were at the time of the survey about 13,000 incorporated places of this size, to say nothing of the unincorporated places and the open country, as compared with fewer than 3,000 places of more than 2,500 population.[14] A survey at the present time would probably show a much larger use of schools in the smaller places because of the growth of consolidated schools, which are much more adaptable to use as community centers than are one-room schools.

In general, the same activities are maintained in rural school centers as in urban school centers. There are, however, certain significant differences in spite of this general similarity. In the survey to which reference has been made, the percentage of schools reporting athletics, clubs and similar groups, social occasions, dancing, night schools, and rooms for quiet games and study was found to be

[12] A school center is defined as a "school which is used regularly at least one evening a week for two or more activities—or twice a week for one—not counting night schools."

[13] E. T. Glueck, *Extended Use of School Buildings*, U. S. Bureau of Education, Bulletin No. 5, 1927, p. 3.

[14] U. S. Bureau of the Census, 15th Census, Vol. 1, p. 14.

significantly higher for urban than for rural communities, while a larger percentage of rural schools reported entertainments, society meetings, and lectures (Table 47).

TABLE 47.—NUMBER AND PER CENT OF SCHOOL CENTERS REPORTING RECREATIONAL ACTIVITIES FOR THE SCHOOL YEAR 1923-1924, BY POPULATION OF TOWNS[a]

Activity	Towns of over 5,000 population		Towns of 2,500–5,000 population		Towns of under 2,500 population	
	Number of school centers	Per cent	Number of school centers	Per cent	Number of school centers	Per cent
Total number of centers reporting..........	1,033	100	164	100	372	100
Athletics................................	745	72	131	80	231	62
Clubs and groups........................	614	59	62	38	119	32
Entertainments..........................	423	41	71	43	212	57
Society meetings.........................	442	43	70	43	192	52
Lectures................................	253	24	44	27	141	38
Social occasions.........................	308	30	47	29	81	22
Civic occasions..........................	241	23	30	18	96	26
Dancing................................	293	28	24	15	21	6
Night schools...........................	249	24	29	18	7	2
Co-operative activities...................	161	16	12	7	41	11
Rooms open for quiet games and study......	165	16	17	10	20	5

[a] Compiled from E. T. Glueck, *Extended Use of School Buildings*, U. S. Bureau of Education, Bulletin No. 5, 1927, Table 10, pp. 12–79.

A significant aspect of the school center movement is its introduction into the rural community of a distinctly urban conception—recreation as a form of social welfare. Formerly in the typical rural community recreation was at best considered only a harmless diversion and at worst was frowned upon as a waste of time. Such recreation as was available was provided by the members of the community themselves and for their own enjoyment. In the school center movement is involved the idea of community welfare and the idea of extending opportunities to an under-privileged group; and those who sponsor the activities do not expect to participate in them on the same basis as those for whom the activities are provided.

[157]

Recreation through Organizations and Associations.—
It is a common misconception that formal organizations
are characteristic only of modern urban life, but there
is ample evidence that formal organizations existed in our
rural communities before the influence of the city began to
be felt. On the other hand, there are certain respects in
which the organizational life of the rural community is to
be distinguished from that of the urban community.
In the first place, rural organizations tend to be general
organizations with a multiplicity of functions, recreation in
particular being combined with other more serious objectives.[15] Rural organizations also tend to be purely local,
in contrast to urban organizations with their tendency to
federate into larger units, most of the important federations
or associations of clubs being distinctly urban, at least in
their development. A third characteristic is closely related
to the question of federation: rural organizations of the
past have usually been of local and spontaneous origin,
while modern urban organizations depend to a much
greater degree upon the initiative and leadership of the
federation headquarters. In all three of these respects, rural
organizations are tending toward the urban pattern.

These trends are all illustrated in the development of
the clubs fostered by the agricultural extension service.
Clubs of this kind all show a tendency toward specialization,
both in function and in membership. Moreover, they, are
federated through the extension service, and their development has been due primarily to the activity of the extension
workers. These clubs are now probably the most typical
organizations to be found in rural communities; in 1930
there were about 35,000 adult home demonstration groups
with nearly 650,000 members and about 56,000 junior
agricultural clubs with 823,000 members.[16] These organizations, however, retain their rural aspect in that the trend

[15] J. H. Kolb and A. F. Wileden *Special Interest Groups in Rural Society,*
University of Wisconsin, Agricultural Experiment Station, Research Bulletin
No. 84, Madison, 1927, p. 15.
[16] U. S. Department of Agriculture, Year Book of Agriculture, 1932, pp. 953,
954.

toward specialization has not as yet isolated recreational interests, recreation still being an important, albeit a secondary, function.

The organizational life of the rural community is also being urbanized by the expansion of urban organizations into rural communities. Statistical data on luncheon clubs illustrate this trend most effectively[17] but the movement is not confined to this type of club, and in fact, the expansion of character-building organizations into rural communities is probably of considerably more importance at the present time. The Young Men's Christian Association began its expansion into rural communities about the beginning of the present century, and by 1928 its Town and Country Department was serving about 1,400 communities, although some of these were small industrial communities rather than agricultural communities.[18] The Young Women's Christian Association undertook rural work much more recently, and this work has not yet reached significant proportions, there being only 47 county or district associations in 1930, with a formal membership of a little more than 46,000.[19] Scouting was introduced to the rural community in 1915 with the establishment of the Lone Scout plan, and since then home or farm patrols have been organized to meet the needs of small groups of boys and regular rural troops have been organized wherever sufficient numbers have been enrolled.[20]

From the standpoint of the process of urbanization, the lodges present something of a puzzle. These organizations experienced their greatest growth before the influence of the cities became dominant, and they became a characteristic feature of practically every rural community. On the other hand, the lodge represents a certain specialization of

[17] No Rotary clubs were organized in towns of less than 5,000 population between 1910 and 1914; on the basis of a random sample, 54 per cent of the Rotary clubs organized between 1925 and 1929 were in places of less than 2,500 population. Similar trends were discovered in the other large luncheon club organizations.
[18] Y. M. C. A. Year Book, 1928.
[19] Correspondence with the National Board of the Y. W. C. A.
[20] Twenty-first Annual Report of the Boy Scouts of America, pp. 192, 193.

function, it is a member of a larger federation, and it has depended to an important degree upon the stimulus of a centralized leadership. But whether the lodge is classified as an urban or as a rural organization, or whether this type of classification is irrelevant, available data indicate the present decline of the lodges in rural communities. An analysis of Masonic membership in Iowa in 1930 indicated that the losses in membership increased as the proportion of the population living on farms increased. Detailed data for other organizations are not available, but it is probable that the trend in the Masonic organization is typical, for the other lodges are either declining in membership for the whole country or are making negligible gains.

Specialized Recreational Facilities in the Rural Community.—In the preceding paragraphs emphasis has been put upon the fact that the provision of recreation has been the function of institutions and organizations established with other primary ends in view. In the city recreation is now very largely a separate department of life. The church, the school, and the numerous associations of the city have to a large degree surrendered their recreational functions, which have been taken over by the parks and playgrounds, the libraries and museums, the theaters, the moving picture houses, the professional athletic organizations, the cabarets and night clubs, and the social and recreational clubs.

Less progress has been made in the urbanization of rural recreation in this respect than in any other, yet a beginning has been made. The facilities designed especially or exclusively for recreation fall naturally into three classes: commercial amusements, public recreational facilities, and the facilities provided by closed groups for their own use, although the last class may be omitted from the discussion of rural recreation.

Commercial recreation is still an urban phenomenon with the exception of the commercial showing of moving pictures.[21] The moving picture theater has, however, very

[21] A correlation between the per capita receipts from amusement taxes in 1920 and the per cent of the population that was rural (by states) yielded a coefficient

[160]

definitely brought commercial recreation to the majority of the rural population. A tabulation of the number of moving picture theaters by geographic divisions reveals the very interesting fact that there is apparently no relation between the population per theater and the proportion of the population living on farms (Table 48). In fact, the

TABLE 48.—NUMBER OF MOTION PICTURE THEATERS IN RELATION TO THE POPULATION, BY GEOGRAPHICAL DIVISIONS, 1929

Geographical division	Number of theaters[a]	Population per theater	Per cent of population living on farms[b]	Population per square mile[c]
United States	23,938	5,129	24.8	41.3
New England	1,330	6,140	7.0	131.8
Middle Atlantic	3,665	7,165	6.5	262.6
East North Central	4,929	5,132	17.7	103.0
West North Central	5,103	2,606	38.1	26.0
South Atlantic	2,440	6,473	37.3	58.7
East South Central	1,297	7,623	51.5	55.1
West South Central	2,204	5,525	43.7	28.3
Mountain	1,283	2,885	30.8	4.3
Pacific	1,687	4,857	14.0	25.8

[a] Compiled from list of theaters in Film Year Book, 1929.
[b] U. S. Bureau of the Census, 15th Census, Population, vol. 3, pt. 1, p. 30.
[c] Ibid., vol. 1, p. 13.

number of theaters relative to the population seems to be more closely related to the density of population, the relative number of theaters decreasing as the density of population increases, indicating that any further increase in the number of theaters must depend upon a growing population rather than upon the introduction of theaters into new communities.

Of growing importance for rural communities is the entertainment now widely available through radio broadcasting stations located in all sections of the country. A tabulation of Kentucky counties according to the per cent of families having radios and the per cent of the population living on

of −.78 ± .04; and a correlation between the per cent of the gainfully employed engaged in recreational occupations in Kentucky counties in 1930 and the per cent of the population living on farms yielded a coefficient of −.64 ± .04.

farms indicates very definitely that the radio has not yet been adopted by rural families to the same extent as it has by urban families. A comparison of the states having large rural populations with those having large urban populations indicates that this relationship probably holds for the country as a whole. In the southern states, in which the rural population is greatest relative to urban population, the per cent of families having radios is low, while in the northern and eastern industrial states the per cent of families having radios is high. The differences between the states, however, cannot be interpreted as due entirely to differences in the per cent of the population that is rural, for some of the southern cities have smaller proportions of the population having radios than do certain rural counties of northern states; in Birmingham, Alabama, for example, 26.7 per cent of the families have radios, the highest ratio for any unit in the state, while in no county in Iowa do less than 32.8 per cent of the families have radios.

Rural communities have made very little public provision for recreation. A large number of agricultural villages have been built around public squares or have otherwise been provided with park space, but because of the freedom from the congested conditions of the large city, these areas have not been of particular recreational significance except as used for band concerts, public festivals, and similar assemblies. Nearly every rural community has had certain places along streams or in woodlands, privately owned, but generally available for picnics and other types of outings. As the value of land has increased, some of these marginal lands have been brought under cultivation and some rural communities have consequently lost, or been threatened with the loss of, these places. A few rural communities, either as groups of private individuals or as governmental units, have purchased such plots of ground to preserve them for recreational purposes.[22] More significant than purely local parks are the state and national parks. The automobile

[22] W. C. Nason, *Rural Planning, the Social Aspects*, U. S. Department of Agriculture, Farmer's Bulletin No. 1325, 1923.

has made these parks accessible to farm families, and while no statistical data are available, comments of observers are to the effect that they are visited by a constantly increasing proportion of farmers.

The public playground as developed in the city is practically unknown to the rural community. Only 73 places of less than 2,500 population are reported in the 1930 Year Book of the National Recreation Association as having made any provision along this line. When it is remembered that several of these represent suburban rather than agricultural areas, and that there are considerably more than 13,000 incorporated places of less than 2,500 population, to say nothing of the unincorporated places, it appears that such public provision for recreation is negligible.

In the community building, the rural community appears to have developed a public recreational facility indigenous to itself, although the rural community building is analogous to such urban centers as Young Men's Christian Association buildings, parish houses, recreational halls provided by industrial concerns, settlement and neighborhood houses, and the like. This movement is very largely confined to the present century. A chart showing the growth in the number of community buildings, given in one of the bulletins of the United States Department of Agriculture, indicates approximately ten buildings in 1900.[23] Recent correspondence with the Department elicited the statement that the number had increased so rapidly in recent years that no attempt was being made to keep a complete record of them. Of 75 community buildings in Montana for which data were available, 68 were erected between 1910 and 1928.[24] The recreational uses of these buildings can be inferred from their equipment. The basic feature is the hall adaptable to use as an auditorium, or for exhibits and fairs, or for dancing or other forms of group activity. Its use as an auditorium is usually

[23] W. C. Nason and C. W. Thompson, *Rural Community Buildings in the United States*, U. S. Department of Agriculture, Bulletin No. 825, 1920, p. 2.
[24] J. W. Barger, *Rural Community Halls in Montana*, University of Montana, Agricultural Experiment Station, Bulletin No. 221, Bozeman 1929, p. 6.

facilitated by the provision of a stage and often dressing rooms and a drop curtain. A kitchen is also a common feature to make possible the use of the hall for banquets and dinners. Other types of equipment include musical instruments, playground and athletic equipment, libraries, and rest rooms.

Because of the very complex character of the influences of the city on rural recreation, it is difficult, if not altogether impossible, to make any summary statement of the degree to which rural recreation has been urbanized. There are, however, two general conclusions to which attention may be called. The first is that the influence of the city on rural recreation so far is more evident in the disappearance of traditional rural amusements than in the appearance of distinctly urban amusements. The second is that the most important urban influences on rural recreation have been those of a non-recreational character. These two generalizations are of course intimately related. That the influence of the city on rural recreation has been largely negative is due to the fact that these non-recreational factors have been of more importance than the mere diffusion of urban recreations. Now that the ground has been cleared, so to speak, in the extensive disappearance of the traditional rural recreations, it may be expected that the actual adoption of urban amusements on the part of the rural population will proceed rather rapidly, a trend which is indeed already noticeable.

CHAPTER IX

THE ADMINISTRATION AND CONTROL OF RECREATION

THE extraordinary expansion of public and commercial recreation during the past few decades has brought with it problems of administration and control which have by no means been satisfactorily solved. Recent years have been a time of experimentation in which many attempts have been made to adjust the functions of government to the demands of modern recreation. The entrance of municipalities into the field of recreation has necessitated the enactment of enabling legislation of various kinds. Governmental bureaus and departments have been established or enlarged to administer public recreational programs. The use of governmental funds for the active promotion of recreation has been contrary to past precedent and has had to make its way in the face of much opposition. The promotion of recreational activities under many different auspices, both public and private, has made it necessary to give attention to problems of coordination. The keener realization of the moral hazards associated with certain forms of commercial amusements has led to efforts to regulate them more strictly in the interests of the general welfare. This role of the government as censor has proved to be a difficult one and many measures have been tried out in the attempt to make its control more effective. These enlarged activities of the government in the two fields of promotion and regulation stand out as one of the important developments in modern recreation.

City Planning and Public Recreation.—One of the serious handicaps faced by municipalities in their efforts to build up an adequate system of public recreation is the general lack of properly located areas that can be used for this purpose. The hit-and-miss manner of growth characteristic of nearly all American cities during last century together with the failure to foresee the requirements of modern recreation precluded any widespread efforts to set aside park lands of sufficient extent to meet future recreational needs. Even with the rise of city planning during the first decade of the present century, little progress was made in this direction, since its first interests were confined largely to the beautification of civic centers and the solution of housing and transportation problems. It was only gradually that city planning commissions responded to the rising tide of interest in sports and games and began including in their official plans recommendations for playgrounds and playfields widely distributed among the residential districts of cities. At the present time comprehensive city plans, which are becoming increasingly common among American cities, include as a matter of course provisions for the extension of public recreation. This step forward is one of the notable achievements of recent years in the field of recreation but the legal authority to put these recommendations into effect has not yet been fully granted to municipalities by state legislatures. The legal powers under which city planning has proceeded have with few exceptions not gone further than to give general authority over the approval of plats set aside for recreation by real estate promoters.[1] Cities for the most part must still depend upon the voluntary cooperation of business interests for new space for public recreation as they extend their outer borders. Fortunately, motives of self-interest as well as of public policy have induced many promoters of new subdivisions to make ample provision for outdoor recreation. Model communities planned with the needs of recreation in mind, such as Radburn, New Jersey, Mariemont, Ohio, and Longview, Washington, point the way to a new type of city in which the dreams of city planners have to a large degree been realized. The replanning, however,

---

[1] A. G. Truxal, *Outdoor Recreation Legislation and Its Effectiveness*, Columbia University Press, 1929, p. 37.

of the older, congested portions of cities so that easily accessible playfields may be available involves sweeping and expensive changes in community structure which do not now seem practicable on a large scale. Nevertheless, the beginnings that have been made in this direction are indications of a new trend which may become more pronounced in the near future.

Changing Legal Status of Municipal Recreation.—During the early period of development of municipally conducted recreation programs, a serious difficulty was the general failure of city charters to give authority to maintain activities of this kind. A few of the large metropolitan centers had been given a sufficient measure of home rule to embark on this new enterprise but it was ordinarily necessary for each city to secure a special act of the state legislature granting the desired permission. Even in states where powers of self government had been granted to cities by state constitutional provision, there was no agreement as to the extent of these powers, and in a number of instances city attorneys rendered adverse decisions when authority was sought to establish municipal recreation. As interest in public recreation developed it became evident that the problem could best be met by working for general state legislation broad enough to confer upon all municipalities the authority to develop recreation in any way that would meet local needs. Enabling acts of this kind covering the field of public recreation were first passed in 1917 and have been actively promoted by the National Recreation Association. This type of permissive legislation has spread gradually and by 1931 twenty-one states had enacted similar laws. In 12 of these states supplementary legislation has recently been passed which provides for the establishment of municipal recreation when it has been voted upon favorably by the people and their approval has been given to the levying of a special tax for its support. This referendum tax legislation has been found to be especially important because of the difficulty in many cases of securing appropriations from the general fund for the support of recreational programs.[2] Since by no means all of the states have passed specific home rule bills covering the field of public recreation, the legal status of this function of city governments is still dependent in many places upon various types of legislation such as acts applying to a single city, powers granted to school boards and park boards, and general police and public welfare powers granted cities by general state codes. The present trend is in the direction of more liberal home rule laws and their broader interpretation so as to include authority to maintain public recreation.[3]

Urban Administrative Agencies.—The administrative direction of the recreational functions of municipalities has varied from city to city and there is not as yet any general agreement concerning the most suitable managing authority. Park boards, playground and recreation commissions, and boards of education are the agencies most frequently charged with responsibility for administering municipal recreational activities. Since urban parks have become important recreation centers, many feel that the park department is the logical place to center control of the recreational system. On the other hand, it is contended that many of the park boards are still too much dominated by earlier traditions of horticultural parks to be in full sympathy with modern recreational developments and therefore are not likely to furnish the kind of leadership needed. For this reason many cities have established recreation boards or commissions whose sole function is to manage the playgrounds and recreation centers operated by the municipality. A third agency is the school board, which has already developed wide responsibilities in the field of recreation through its administration of school community centers and school playgrounds, and, in the opinion of many, should extend this phase of its work to include whatever recreational facilities the city

[2] Arthur Williams, "Twenty-five Years of Progress in Recreation Legislation," *Recreation*, 25: 80–81 (1931).
[3] A. G. Truxal, *Outdoor Recreation Legislation and Its Effectiveness*, Columbia University Press, 1929, ch. 1.

ADMINISTRATION AND CONTROL

may provide. More than three-fourths of the governmental agencies administering municipal recreation belong to these three classes, according to reports made to the National Recreation Association (Table 49). Other gov-

TABLE 49.—GOVERNMENTAL AGENCIES ADMINISTERING PUBLIC RECREATION IN CITIES, 1921, 1926, 1931[a]

Governmental agency	Number of agencies reporting		
	1921	1926	1931
Park commissions, boards, departments, committees......................	58[b]	127[b]	228[d]
Playground and recreation commissions, boards, departments..............	88[c]	197[c]	200
Boards of education and other school authorities.........................	128	124	167[e]
Mayors, city councils, city managers, borough authorities.................	11	10	74
Park and recreation commissions, boards, departments....................	....	....	29
Municipal playground committees, associations, and advisory commissions...	....	....	30[f]
Departments of public works...	6	10	18
Departments of parks and public property or buildings....................	4	....	13
Departments of public welfare..	3	5	9
Departments of finance and revenue....................................	....	....	3
Water departments..	....	....	2
Departments of public safety...	....	....	3
Swimming pool commissions...	....	....	2
Other departments..	8	6	11

[a] Year Book of the National Recreation Association, 1931. *Recreation*, June, 1932.
[b] Includes Park and Recreation Commissions.
[c] Includes many subordinate recreation divisions and bureaus.
[d] Sixteen of these park authorities are in Chicago and New York.
[e] Increase due to additional school reports received in connection with school recreation study.
[f] These authorities administered recreation facilities and programs financed by municipal funds, although in some of the cities it is probable that they were not municipally appointed.

ernmental agencies less frequently placed in charge of recreation are city councils, mayors, city managers, departments of public works, departments of public welfare, departments of finance and revenue, departments of public safety, and other city authorities. In some cases also two or more municipal agencies combine in the management of recreation facilities and programs. While no marked trends are noticeable, the recent growth of departments of recreation is significant since it seems to indicate a fuller recognition of the value of this comparatively new governmental function. The progressive leadership of these independent departments appears from the fact that

[169]

more than one-half of the cities in which such departments operate employ at least one worker for full-time recreation service throughout the year. On the other hand, in cities where other authorities are in control, full time recreation workers are much more seldom employed.[4]

Administration of State Recreation.—The activities of the states in the field of recreation are found chiefly in connection with their administration of state parks, forests, and wild game preserves. The administrative control of these state lands varies from state to state, the managing authority sometimes being a park board, the forestry department, department of public works, department of conservation, or a fish and game commission. In 1922 the National Conference on State Parks undertook to draft a model state park law but on account of the different requirements of the states it made only general recommendations looking toward a more uniform administration through the establishment of a state board of park commissioners. The most recent tendency has been in the direction of the more centralized control of parks, forests, and game preserves through departments of conservation. This movement to coordinate the work of these different state agencies by placing all under the direction of a single governmental authority has gone forward most notably in the states of Indiana, Michigan, Wisconsin, New Jersey, and California.[5]

The methods of acquisition and maintenance of state parks vary considerably in the different states. Direct appropriations, bond issues, revenues derived from fish and game licenses, rentals of camp sites, concessions, and admission charges are the usual sources of state park funds. In order to facilitate the acquirement of suitable sites for state parks the right of eminent domain is sometimes conferred on park authorities. It has been through private gifts and donations, however, that these state recreation areas have made their greatest expansion in some of the states. This

[4] Year Book of the National Recreation Association, *Recreation*, June, 1931.
[5] A. G. Truxal, *Outdoor Recreation Legislation and Its Effectiveness*, Columbia University Press, 1929, pp. 102–105.

large dependence upon private contributions has in the opinion of some leaders hindered the proper development of state recreation by creating the impression that it is not a fully recognized state activity. During recent years the people in several states have given their approval to the issuance of bonds for the acquirement of state parks and forests and the trend seems to be towards a more adequate program of state recreation.[6]

Federal Recreation Trends.—While the federal government is not directly concerned with the promotion of recreation, the national parks, national monuments, and national forests constitute a major recreational resource of great value and wide use. The responsibility for the administration of these federal lands is divided among several departments. The national parks are administered by the National Park Service of the Department of the Interior; the national monuments by the National Park Service, Department of Agriculture, and the War Department; and the national forests by the Department of Agriculture. All these federal agencies look favorably upon the increasing recreational use of these federal lands and are endeavoring to administer them in such a manner as to facilitate their enjoyment by the public. Nevertheless, their primary purpose is not to furnish facilities for outdoor recreation. The national parks were established to preserve areas of unique scenic interest and additional parks can be added to the federal system only when they come up to the standards of beauty set up by the national authorities. The national forests were created for the purpose of bringing about a wiser utilization of their timber resources. The Forest Service is not engaged in the task of preserving the forests as a permanent recreational asset but in preventing their unwise exploitation by private interests. For these reasons, the authorities charged with the control of these federal lands can adopt recreational policies only in so far as they do not conflict with the major purposes for which these reservations were originally made.

[6] Beatrice W. Nelson, *State Recreation*, National Conference on State Parks, Inc. 1928, pp. 11–18.

In view of the growing demand for more extensive out-door recreational facilities, it has been proposed that the federal government create a special bureau or commission whose sole function shall be the building up of a public recreational program. Others believe that the situation can be adequately met by setting up machinery for the coordination of the various recreational activities of the existing federal bureaus and departments.[7] There is now no strong movement in the direction of federal promotion of recreation beyond the present efforts on the part of the federal administrative authorities to develop better facilities for the recreational use of lands under their control.

Governmental Support of Public Recreation.—The shift from voluntary to governmental support of public recreation is one of the significant changes that have taken place during the past thirty years. At the beginning of the modern recreation movement private leadership was at the helm and little encouragement was given to those who sought the cooperation of public authorities. The first playgrounds were conducted by private agencies and financed by private funds. Public recreation during its early period of development took its place along side of other welfare activities maintained by philanthropic organizations. In spite of widespread opposition the early recreation leaders took the position that the provision of public recreation should be a governmental function and vigorous efforts were made to build up a public opinion that would support such a policy. Public school systems were urged to turn over their playgrounds to the community for use when the schools were not in session. Pressure was brought to bear upon municipal park boards to permit the free use of parks for games and sports. Chicago gave a powerful impetus to municipal recreation through a $5,000,000 bond issue approved in 1903 by the voters of the South Park

[7] R. S. Yard, "The Scenic Resources of the United States," *The Playground*, 18: 214. Barrington Moore, "Outlines of A National Outdoor Recreational Policy with Special Reference to the Work of Federal Agencies," *The Playground*, 18: 216. J. H. Pratt, "Elements of a Federal Recreation Policy," *The Playground*, 18: 225.

District for the purpose of establishing additional parks. Turning aside from past precedents, the South Park Commissioners utilized this money in building up small parks as playfields and recreation centers equipped with field houses and facilities for both outdoor and indoor play. In the other large metropolitan centers a similar development took place which gradually spread to the smaller cities. During the second and third decades of the present century this movement toward municipal support of public recreation went forward with great rapidity. Municipal appropriations in increasing amounts have been made for the construction of athletic fields, swimming pools, bathing beaches, golf courses, and other recreational facilities, and public opinion generally gives its approval to the expenditure of public funds for these purposes (Table 50). In 1931, 672 cities

TABLE 50.—PER CAPITA EXPENDITURES OF CITIES OF 30,000 POPULATION OR MORE AND OF STATES FOR THE OPERATION AND MAINTENANCE OF RECREATION DEPARTMENTS AND OF ALL GENERAL DEPARTMENTS, 1915–1928[a]

Year	Cities		States	
	Recreation departments	All departments	Recreation departments	All departments
1915....................	$0.68	$18.45	$0.01	$ 3.85
1917....................	0.66	18.96	0.01	4.19
1919....................	0.74	21.63	0.01	5.16
1922....................	1.09	33.15	0.02	8.48
1924....................	1.15	35.61	0.02	9.00
1926....................	1.34	38.99	0.03	8.98
1927....................	1.40	40.77	0.03	9.55
1928....................	1.44	42.43	0.03	10.18

[a] U. S. Bureau of the Census, *Financial Statistics of Cities*, 1928, p. 50, and *Financial Statistics of States*, 1928, p. 27.

reported the expenditure of tax funds for public recreation while 118 cities reported that their recreational activities were supported by private funds only (Table 51). During this same year, according to reports made to the National Recreation Association, 90 per cent of the expenditures for public recreation came from tax funds, 7 per cent from fees

TABLE 51.—SOURCES OF SUPPORT OF PUBLIC RECREATON IN CITIES, 1921, 1926, 1931[a]

Source of support	Number of cities reporting		
	1921	1926	1931
Municipal funds	244	392	672
Municipal and private funds	120	221	149
Private funds	135	139	118
County funds	...	3	53
Miscellaneous public funds	1	...	1
Miscellaneous public and private funds	2	3	4

[a] Year Book of the National Recreation Association, 1931. *Recreation*, 26: 30 (1931).

and charges, and 3 per cent from private contributions.[8] The lag in the trend toward municipal support of recreation is most noticeable in the small cities and towns where the need of public recreation does not seem to be so keenly felt. In some of these municipalities private recreational agencies are still at work but in general the activities of the latter are now mainly of an experimental or pioneering nature with the intention of shifting their burden to governmental agencies as soon as this becomes possible. Public recreation as a proper function of government is now generally accepted but it apparently is only in the early stages of its development. The present trend is toward a wider provision of public recreational facilities not merely by municipalities but by other local units of government.

Regulation and Control of Commercial Amusements.— The role of the government as supervisor and censor of commercial amusements antedates by far its more recently assumed functions of public recreation promotion. The close relationship between amusements and morals and the tendency to increase financial profits by providing demoralizing forms of popular entertainment have made it necessary for the public to set up standards and regulations in the interests of the general welfare. These efforts to control commercial amusements have resulted in the enactment of laws and ordinances which the various branches of the

[8] *Recreation,* 26: 60 (1931).

government are called upon to enforce. This supervisory function of the government has always presented many serious difficulties and the problem of effective regulation is apparently as far as ever from a satisfactory solution.

One of the forms of commercial amusements that has been especially difficult to regulate is the public dance hall. Prior to the outbreak of the World War there was no widespread effort to control the operation of these places of amusement although it was well known that they were frequently associated with saloons and tended in many instances to exert a demoralizing influence upon their patrons. Beyond the enactment of occasional laws forbidding the attendance of young people below a certain age, little progress was made in securing regulatory legislation. Public inspection of dance halls was seldom made and when officers of the law attended these places, their presence was designed primarily to prevent acts of serious disorder. The publication of surveys exposing dance hall evils, together with the effort during the World War to provide wholesome recreation for those in military training, led to more aggressive efforts to bring this form of amusement under public control. It is estimated that 75 per cent of the existing dance hall ordinances of the more complete type have been passed since 1918. In 1928 there were 28 states which had enacted laws dealing specifically with the regulation of public dances and dance halls and practically all the states had conferred full power upon municipalities to license and control these places of amusement.[9]

Recently enacted dance hall legislation seeks to accomplish its purpose through the requirement of licenses which are to be given only to halls that maintain certain required standards and comply with regulations convering such matters as hours of closing, participation of minors, lighting of premises, and conduct of dancers. Provision is also made for official supervision, a task frequently delegated to specially appointed matrons or police women. In cities

[9] Ella Gardner, *Public Dance Halls*, Children's Bureau Publication No. 189, 1929, pp. 1–10.

where public opinion has supported the enforcement of these laws, the situation has materially improved. Especially is this true of the large and more attractive ball rooms where the management is desirous of securing a good class of patrons. The closed or taxi-dance hall presents a different kind of problem and little success has attended efforts either to abolish it or to conduct it in such a manner that it would not be a demoralizing influence. The same is true of the road houses and night clubs located outside of city limits and therefore free from the supervision of city authorities. Even where state laws provide for the regulation of these amusement places, the lack of enforcement officers makes it impracticable to put these laws into effect. In spite of all the difficulties faced in the attempt to control dance halls in the interests of public morals, the past decade has been a period of wide enactment of stricter laws, and public opinion in many places insists upon a careful supervision of these places of amusement.

Another form of commercial amusement over which society has sought to exercise control is the motion picture. The widely prevailing belief that motion pictures strongly influence conduct has led to various efforts to censor films in order to prevent the public showing of those deemed to be vulgar or indecent or of a type that might incite to crime. One of the first efforts to deal with this problem was made by the city of Chicago in 1907 when responsibility was placed upon the chief of police for the issuance of motion picture permits.[10] Since one of the duties of the police is to regulate all performances that may be regarded as injurious to the public welfare, this type of ordinance, which served as a pattern for some other cities, was a natural adaptation of the existing machinery of local government to the problem at hand. This method of control through a licensing system operated by the police department has been subjected to serious criticism and in some places has been supplanted by the appointment of official censorship boards. Kansas City, Missouri, in 1913 made one of the first experi-

[10] M. R. Davie, *Problems of City Life*, 1932, p. 615.

ments in this direction by creating the office of Censor of Films and Pictures with power to appoint an official board of censors. Municipal censorship boards were established later by other cities but this method of dealing with the problem did not become widespread. In 1926 it was estimated that less than 100 cities had provided officially appointed censorship boards or officials.[11]

While these attempts at local control of motion pictures have performed some service, the wide variations in standards in different municipalities have been very confusing and unsatisfactory to the general public and subject the producers to a great deal of expense in modifying the films to suit the requirements of each city in which they are shown. A beginning has been made in the direction of more centralized control of this problem by setting up state machinery in the following states: Pennsylvania, Ohio, Kansas, Maryland, New York, Virginia, and Florida. This state legislation, which has been enacted between 1911 and 1922, usually provides for a censorship board whose approval must be obtained before films can be exhibited within the state. The one exception is Florida, which has no censorship board of its own but prohibits the showing of any film not approved by the National Board of Review or by the Motion Picture Commission of the State of New York. Two other states have brought about the censorship of films by indirect means: Massachusetts by making it necessary for all films shown on Sunday to be licensed by the Commissioner of Public Safety, and Connecticut by requiring the registration of films and the payment of a tax with power given to the Tax Commissioner to revoke the registration of any picture that he may find to be objectionable. State censorship bills have been introduced in many other states but have not been acted upon favorably.[12]

The failure of many states to enact state censorship legislation has given strength to the efforts to get Congress

---

[11] F. H. MacGregor, "Official Censorship Legislation," *The Annals*, 128: 170.
[12] *Ibid.*, pp. 166–169.

to place censorship of motion pictures under national control. Among the bills introduced during the past twenty years for the purpose of accomplishing this end, the more important have provided for the creation of a Federal Motion Picture Commission as a division of the Office of Education of the Department of the Interior. To this Commission was to be given power not merely to preview and license all films but also to censor scenarios and to supervise their production in studios. While this proposed legislation attracted considerable attention throughout the country, it was never able to marshall enough votes to secure its passage. The most important federal legislation having to do with motion pictures is the law passed in 1912 making interstate traffic in prize-fight films unlawful. This law, however, has been easy to evade and has never been widely enforced.[13]

Contrary to the practice of most foreign countries, official censorship of moving pictures has never been popular in this country and has made comparatively little progress. In spite of the fact that the constitutionality of censorship legislation has been established in the highest courts, the people have not been able to agree upon any wide reaching official plan for the control of motion picture exhibitions. Many believe that official censorship can deal only with the more flagrant violations of our moral code and that this purpose can be accomplished more effectively by bringing pressure to bear upon the motion picture industry to produce a better type of films. The trend in this country is not toward a wider development of censorship laws but rather toward greater reliance upon the efforts of voluntary agencies to build up community standards and develop a public opinion that will demand the production of motion pictures of the highest order.

Control through Suppression.—A much more serious problem is faced when the government goes beyond its usual task of supervision and regulation and undertakes to suppress amusements that violate the social code or are

[13] M. R. Davie, *Problems of City Life*, 1932, p. 615.

regarded as dangerous to public morals. There is no lack of legislation prohibiting such amusements but its enforcement by the police and other government officials is extremely difficult. The long and futile efforts of the government to suppress gaming devices, gambling in connection with legitimate amusements, and resorts that foster vice and immorality are matters of common knowledge and represent a serious breakdown of the forces of law and order. Illegal amusements for which there is a considerable popular demand have always flourished in spite of governmental opposition and apparently the same situation prevails today in American municipalities.[14] From time to time reform movements are inaugurated, a new administration may come into power, and as a result illegal amusements are forced to run for cover, but such victories are never final or complete, and it is doubtful whether any great headway has been made in recent years in bringing about a satisfactory solution of this perplexing problem.

The effort to control through suppression is seen also in the movement to prohibit Sunday amusements. Legislation restricting both work and play on the Sabbath became quite general during colonial times and still appears in various forms in the legal codes of most of the states. While legislation of this kind, in so far as it applies to sports and amusements, is generally regarded as obsolete, these blue laws have not been widely repealed and in some sections of the country, notably in several of the eastern and southern states, the government undertakes more or less vigorously to bring about their enforcement. In the cities of largest size, recreation parks and playgrounds and amusement places generally operate freely the entire week but in many of the smaller cities and towns Sunday closing of such places is required. A recent survey of a small but representative group of cities of 50,000 population or less showed that 36 cities kept their public recreation centers open although leadership was provided in only 19, and that 32 cities kept

[14] Article on "Public Amusements," *Encyclopaedia of the Social Sciences,* Vol. 2: 45.

such recreation places closed. The general trend of public sentiment in most places was found to be in the direction of a wider use of recreational facilities on Sunday.[15] In some cities the growing demand for Sunday amusements has led to the enactment of more liberal legislation, as for example in Baltimore where the old blue laws were recently repealed to the extent of legalizing sports and amusements after 2 o'clock Sunday afternoons. Much more frequently the same purpose is achieved through lax enforcement of Sunday laws allowed to remain on the statute books. The failure of law enforcement agencies to suppress Sunday amusements has never been more widespread than at the present time and seems to indicate a definite turning of the tide of public opinion away from the earlier ideas of Sunday observance.

[15] C. A. Emmons, Jr., "Sunday Recreation," *American City*, April, 1931, p. 135.

Chapter X

EXPENDITURES FOR RECREATION

THE first difficulty confronted when an attempt is made to compute the cost of recreation is that of determining the items to be included. Recreation is by no means a clearly defined field but shades off into borderline areas and becomes intermingled with activities of many diverse kinds. Work and play frequently go hand in hand and cannot always be readily separated. People travel in the interests of both pleasure and business. There are many organizations that combine recreational activities with the promotion of a serious program. The consumption of luxuries is closely associated with leisure time activities and from one point of view their cost might be included in the recreational budget. An equally important question arises concerning the inclusion of pleasures and leisure time avocations proscribed by law. For purposes of this chapter the estimate of expenditures has been confined to those general classes of activities that have been previously discussed. Such items as candy, chewing gum, non-alcoholic beverages, food consumed at banquets and entertainments, tobacco, liquor, prostitution, and gambling as well as many of the luxuries that are intimately connected with the enjoyment of leisure have been excluded. There have been omitted also for the most part the intellectual and cultural leisure time pursuits such as reading, music, art, and other activities of a similar nature. Attention has been chiefly centered upon sports, games, pleasure travel, amusements, clubs, leisure time associations, all of which enjoy social approval and fall directly rather than indirectly within the field of recreation.

In addition to the problems growing out of the ill-defined limits of the field is the unsatisfactory nature of much of the data that must be relied upon in estimating costs. At the start we are confronted by a most discouraging lack of sources, an obstacle in itself which places the most serious limitations upon a study of this kind. Comprehensive figures for the entire country cannot be secured for all recreational activities. The cost of some items must be estimated on the basis of scattered data which may not be entirely representative of the total situation. Some of the sources are of such a nature that the amount of overlapping and duplication cannot be determined. Unfortunately there is no way of making an accurate estimate of the cost of the informal visiting and entertaining which constitute a large share of the recreation of millions of people. Expenditures for pleasure travel must be computed from the total cost of travel and are merely estimates about which there may not be general agreement. Because of the difficulties involved, it has been impracticable in all cases to include a proportionate allowance for capital investment in addition to current expenditures.

The nature of the data has made it advisable to state the expenditures for recreation in round numbers. These approximations, however, have been arrived at through a careful study of available sources, and the general estimates used are only those issued by competent authorities. An effort has been made to present a minimum rather than a maximum cost of recreation. In cases of doubt estimates have been reduced to a more conservative figure. It is believed that the items omitted, or only partially included because of lack of data, more than compensate for any overlapping in the figures given or overstatements in regard to any particular class of expenditures. An effort was made to secure data for the year 1930 but it was found necessary to rely upon figures for 1928 and 1929 for some of the items. For this reason the totals arrived at should be regarded merely as a general estimate of the recent annual cost of recreation rather than as a statement for the year 1930 (Table 52).

Estimated Total Expenditures.—The annual expenditure of more than ten billion dollars for recreation, according to

TABLE 52.—ESTIMATED ANNUAL COST OF RECREATION[a]

(In thousands of dollars)

	Amount of expenditures	
A. Governmental expenditures:		
1. Municipalities	$ 147,179	
2. Counties	8,600	
3. States	28,331	
4. Federal	9,300	
Total		$ 193,410
B. Travel and mobility:		
1. Vacation travel in the United States—		
(a) Automobile touring	3,200,000	
(b) Travel by rail	750,000	
(c) Travel by air and water	25,000	
2. Vacation travel abroad—		
(a) To Canada	266,283	
(b) To Mexico	55,642	
(c) To countries overseas	391,470	
(d) To insular possessions	1,326	
(e) Alien American tourists abroad	76,000	
3. Pleasure-use of cars, boats, etc.—		
(a) Automobiles (except touring)	1,246,000	
(b) Motor boats	460,000	
(c) Motor cycles	10,796	
(d) Bicycles	9,634	
Total		6,492,151
C. Commercial amusements:		
1. Moving pictures	1,500,000	
2. Other admissions	166,000	
3. Cabarets and night clubs	23,725	
4. Radios and radio broadcasting	525,000	
Total		2,214,725
D. Leisure time associations:		
1. Social and athletic clubs	125,000	
2. Luncheon clubs	7,500	
3. Lodges	175,000	
4. Youth service and similar organizations	75,000	
Total		382,500
E. Games, sports, outdoor life, etc.:		
1. Toys, games, playground equipment	113,800	
2. Pool, billiards, bowling equipment	12,000	
3. Playing cards	20,000	
4. Sporting and athletic goods	500,000	
5. Hunting and fishing licenses	12,000	
6. College football	21,500	
7. Resort hotels	75,000	
8. Commercial and other camps	47,000	
9. Fireworks	6,771	
10. Phonographs and accessories	75,000	
Total		883,071
Total annual cost of recreation		$10,165,857

[a] The figures in this table are for the most part for the year 1930 but in some instances the latest figures available were for the years 1928 and 1929. The table therefore does not apply to any single year but may be regarded as an estimate of the annual cost of recreation at the end of the past decade before the effects of the financial depression began to be seriously felt.

the figures given in Table 52, gives some indication of the extensive role of leisure time activities in the lives of the American people. However huge may seem this sum, it is less than half the amount recently estimated by Stuart Chase to be our bill for play. His figures, which total $21,045,000,000, include expenditures for such items as newspapers, tabloids, light fiction (in part), pleasure use of telephone, entertaining and visiting, candy, chewing gum, hard and soft drinks (in part), tobacco (in part), collections, hobbies, celebrations, commissions on gambling, etc., all of which have been omitted from the present estimate. When the cost of these items is deducted, his estimate amounts to $11,830,000,000, which fairly closely approximates the figures given in this chapter.[1]

The recreational expenditures included in this discussion have been divided into five general classes:.governmental expenditures, travel and mobility, commercial amusements leisure-time associations, and a miscellaneous group of games, sports, camping, etc. When classified in this manner, travel stands out as the most expensive recreational activity with commercial amusements occupying second place. The cost of games, sports, and outdoor life, when supplemented by governmental expenditures which are largely for this purpose, amount to more than a billion dollars and stand third in this list of recreational expenses. While in this compilation of costs it has not been possible rigidly to separate active and passive forms of amusement, it is quite evident that the bulk of our recreational expenditures, contrary to the opinion of many people, must be charged against forms of leisure time pursuits in which the people actively participate.

---

[1] Stuart Chase, "Play," in C. A. Beard's *Whither Mankind*, Longmans, Green and Co., 1928, ch. 14. Other recent but less comprehensive estimates of the cost of recreation are: Arthur B. Reeve, "What America Spends for Sport," *Outing*, 57: 300–308 (1910); W. R. Ingalls, *Wealth and Income of the American People*, A Survey of the Economic Consequences of the War, York, Pa., 1922, pp. 216–218; George B. Cutten, *The Threat of Leisure*, Yale University Press, 1926, p. 70–71; Henry S. Curtis, "Can America Afford an Adequate System of Playgrounds?" *The American City*, July 1927, pp. 65–66.

Governmental Expenditures.—The total expenditures of the various branches of the government for the promotion of recreation, computed from the most recent available data, amount to $193,410,000, 76 per cent of which was spent by municipalities, 15 per cent by states, 5 per cent by the federal government, and 4 per cent by counties. Figures covering municipal expenditures for recreation are accessible only for cities of 30,000 population or more since cities of smaller size are not included in the *Financial Statistics of Cities* issued by the Bureau of the Census. According to the 1928 edition of this census report, the 250 cities estimated to have populations in excess of 30,000 at that time expended $62,871,000 for the operation and maintenance of public recreational facilities and $73,018,890 for outlay for new properties. When to these sums are added the interest payments on debts incurred for recreational purposes, the total municipal expenditures for recreation in these 250 cities amounted to $147,179,000. The total value of the recreational property in these cities was $2,405,572,-000, which constituted 36 per cent of the value of all municipal property exclusive of public service enterprises. The value of property for recreational use was exceeded only by the value of school property. The gross expenditures of the different states for recreation during 1928 totaled $28,331,000, which includes the cost of operating the recreation departments, expenditures for fish and game conservation, and outlays for new parks, reservations, etc., together with the proportionate interest payments on debts.[2] The computation of federal expenditures for recreation is a difficult matter since these are not reported separately by the census bureau as is done for cities and states. Various federal bureaus and departments are engaged in some form of recreational promotion but the expenditures for these purposes cannot be easily segregated. The only items included in this estimate of federal expenditures are the national parks, the bird, fish, and wild life refuges, fish and game protection, recreation and land use

[2] U. S. Bureau of the Census, *Financial Statistics of States*, 1928.

of the Forest Service, and the Federal Radio Commission. For these items the federal government expended, in 1930, $9,300,000, four-fifths of which was required for the maintenance of the national parks.[3]

Travel and Mobility.—In arriving at an estimate of the cost of vacation travel within the United States, use has been made of the figures given out by the Research Department of the American Automobile Association. According to their estimates for 1930, $3,200,000,000 was spent by Americans on vacation motor tours, $750,000,000 for vacation travel by rail, and $25,000,000 for vacation travel by air and water.[4] The United States Department of Commerce issues each year a bulletin dealing with the balance of international payments of the United States, in which detailed estimates are given of the expenditures of American tourists abroad. For the year 1930 these expenditures approximated $790,721,000, half of which was spent by American tourists over seas. The amount spent by American tourists in Canada was $266,283,000, which was more than one-third of the total spent in foreign travel.[5]

In addition to the expenditures of auto tourists given above, there is also the cost of the pleasure use of the automobile for short trips. The estimate of $1,246,000,000 to cover this important item was computed in the following manner. If we accept $350 as the average annual cost of operation per passenger car (including depreciation, interest on investment, and general upkeep), the expenditures for the 21,554,000 passenger cars estimated to have been in actual use in 1930 amount to $7,544,000,000. This amount does not seem excessive in view of the fact that it represents a rate of 5 cents for each mile of automobile travel on the assumption that passenger cars are on the average driven 7,000 miles a year. Just how much of this total expenditure

[3] U. S. Treasury Department, *Combined Statement of Receipts and Expenditures, Balances, etc. of the United States, 1930.*

[4] *Recreational Travel in 1930,* Research Department of the American Automobile Association, Washington, D. C.

[5] U. S. Department of Commerce, *The Balance of International Payments of the United States in 1930.*

for the operation of motor cars should be charged against their recreational use is difficult to determine. It may be conservatively estimated, in view of recent traffic surveys, that at least one-fourth of the use of passenger cars is for recreation. On this basis we have $1,886,000,000 to cover the total amount spent on motor cars during 1930 for both touring and short pleasure trips. Since 20 per cent of the cost of motor touring, as given in the above estimate of the American Automobile Association, represents charges for car operation, $640,000,000 was deducted from $1,886,000,000 which leaves $1,246,000,000 as the approximate amount spent for the daily pleasure use of the automobile exclusive of touring. While the total costs of the recreational use of the automobile amount to an extraordinary figure, the estimates have been made on a conservative basis and are probably well within the facts.

The value of motorcycles, side cars and parts, according to the reports of the 1929 census of manufactures, was $10,796,000. Unfortunately there is no way of determining to what extent motorcycles are used for recreational travel. In the present estimate, the manufactured value of these cars has been regarded as the total cost of motorcycling for pleasure on the assumption that the higher price paid for the machines by the consumer plus the cost of upkeep is approximately equal to the value of the machines used primarily for business purposes.

The census of manufactures places the value of bicycles and bicycle parts produced in 1929 at $9,634,000. Bicycles are used predominantly but of course not exclusively for pleasure. This value of the bicycle at the factory has been taken as the cost of the pleasure use of the bicycle, although it is probably an underestimate in view of the wide difference between the manufacturer's value and the retail value of the bicycles manufactured.[6]

Commercial Amusements.—The task of estimating the total expenditures for commercial amusements cannot be carried out satisfactorily because there is no centralized

[6] *United States Census of Manufactures,* 1929.

[187]

method of reporting amounts paid for admission to amusement places except those subject to taxation. During and immediately following the World War, when practically all commercial amusements were taxed, it was possible to estimate fairly accurately the expenditures in this field. In 1924, when admissions as low as ten cents were subject to federal taxation, the total amount paid by the public for admission to places required to pay this tax was approximately $768,000,000. This doubtless included moving picture and other theaters, concerts given for financial profit, baseball and other games, amusement parks, etc. The federal tax on amusements of this class for the year 1930 applied only to admissions of three dollars or more and therefore is of no value in computing the total amount spent on such amusements that year. In 1928, when admissions of more than 75 cents were taxed one cent for each ten cents or fraction thereof, the amount spent for admissions to places subject to this tax was somewhere near $166,000,-000.[7] Since few motion picture theaters during that year charged an admission above 75 cents, this estimate for admissions to theaters, concerts, exhibitions, etc. may be regarded as an expenditure additional to the amount spent on motion pictures. This amount, which has been used as our estimate of admissions other than moving pictures, is doubtless too conservative inasmuch as it does not include the large sum that must have been expended for admission charges less than 75 cents at many different kinds of amusement places.

Another class of commercial amusements taxed by the federal government is listed under the heading of cabarets, roof gardens, etc. The government tax is 20 per cent of the total charge made by these places, on the assumption that this proportion of the expenditure goes for entertainment while the remaining 80 per cent is paid for the food. This tax, at the rate of one and one-half cents for each ten cents or fraction thereof, yielded a revenue of $711,752 in 1930. Assuming a straight tax of 15 per cent, the 20 per cent of the

[7] Annual Reports of the United States Commissioner of Internal Revenue.

total charges that were taxed amounted to $4,745,000, and the total charge to $23,725,000. Since the primary motive in attending a resort of this class is to enjoy the entertainment, it seems proper to include the total charge in figuring the cost of recreation.

The amount spent on admissions to motion picture theaters is estimated to be $1,500,000,000.[8] This is computed on the basis of 100,000,000 admissions per week at an average admission price of 30 cents. This estimate of motion picture expenditures is perhaps too low, for the weekly attendance during 1930 very probably approximated 115,000,000 and 40 cents may not be too high for the average price of admission that year. If these latter figures are used as a basis for computation, the annual expenditures by the public for motion pictures would be $2,392,000,000.

Radios and radio parts cost the American people in 1930 approximately $500,951,000, a marked decline over the sales made during the preceding year. The cost of broadcasting programs paid indirectly by the public through advertisers was at least $25,000,000.[9] If to these items a reasonable charge is added for the upkeep of the 12,000,000 radios in use throughout the country, it is apparent that the estimate of $525,000,000 as the expenditures for radio entertainment during 1930 is very conservative.

It is probable that the above items cover the major expenditures for commercial amusements although no account has been taken of such items as pool and billiard halls, penny arcades, street carnivals, amusement parks and other amusement places where the admission charge is too small to be subject to federal taxation. The total estimate of $2,214,725,000 should be regarded as a minimum and not a maximum expenditure in this important field of recreation.

Leisure Time Associations.—Expenditures for the support of private organizations in the field of leisure have

[8] Estimates of attendance made by the Motion Picture Producers and Distributors of America.
[9] Martin Codel, "Radio and Its Future," *Harpers*, 1930, pp. 203–204. National Advertising Records, January 1931.

been computed only for four major types of associations for which reasonably satisfactory data are available. Clubs and associations maintained primarily for purposes of recreation are subject to federal taxation when their dues are more than $25 a year. The income of clubs that fall within this class, computed from the federal taxes paid, must have amounted to more than $125,000,000 in 1930.[10] This includes all the largest and most important recreational associations such as country, golf, tennis, yacht, and other sport clubs, but there are an unknown number of small clubs within this group that escape taxation since their annual dues are $25 or less. Luncheon clubs and fraternal societies are exempt from government taxation since they have functions in addition to the provision of recreation for their members. The luncheon club members, who number approximately 500,000, must pay in annual dues $7,500,000 on the basis of $15 per member, which is the minimum dues for the federations having more than half the membership of luncheon clubs.[11] A careful analysis of the data on secret societies and fraternal organizations shows that the membership in 1930 was about 35,000,000. If membership dues average $5 a year, which is a low estimate, the total spent on these organizations that year was $175,000,000. Another important type of association is the Youth Service Associations and other organizations interested in providing better recreational facilities for the general public. Considering only the largest and best known of associations of this class, their total yearly expenditures amount to about $75,000,-000. The grand total of $382,500,000 for associations in the leisure time field is a minimum estimate since there are other types of organizations that might have been included.

Games, Sports, Outdoor Life, Etc.—According to data supplied by the United States Department of Commerce, the production of sporting and athletic goods, including firearms, ammunition, sport clothing, etc., in 1929 approximated $350,000,000. Exports of these commodities exceeded

[10] Annual Report of the United States Commissioner of Internal Revenue, 1930.
[11] Data supplied by the headquarters of luncheon club federations.

imports by $8,000,000, reducing the value of goods for sale in this country to $342,000,000. It is estimated that the cost of these goods to the consumer was at least $500,000,-000. Doll carriages, go-carts, velocipedes, tricycles, children's wagons and automobiles, sleds, mechanical toys, dolls, play furniture, and playground equipment represent an expenditure of about $113,000,000 based on the value of these goods at the factory. Computed in the same manner the cost of phonographs and accessories amount to $75,000,-000. Expenditures for pool, billiard, and bowling equipment totaled $12,000,000; for fireworks, $6,700,000. Federal tax during 1930 was paid on 48,000,000 packs of playing cards, the retail value of which must have been at least $20,000,000 during 1930. Approximately 100,000 persons attend the 1,350 commercial camps, and their expenditures at an average of $300 per person amount to $30,000,000. The 1,140,000 persons who attended in 1929 the summer camps maintained by welfare organizations, spent $17,000,-000 if the average expenditure per person was $15. Admissions to college football games amounted in 1930 to approximately $21,500,000. Guests at summer and winter resort hotels, according to the 1930 hotel census, spent about $75,000,000.[12]

The Mounting Costs of Recreation.—It is quite clear from the evidence presented in the preceding chapters that the cost of recreation reached a high level at the close of the past decade that had never before been attained. A certain part of this advancing cost was brought about by increasing numbers and expanding wealth and should be regarded merely as a normal accompaniment of a growing nation. But by far the largest share of this advance, especially during the past ten or fifteen years, is the result of a new popular interest in recreation that has revolutionized

[12] U. S. Department of Commerce, Bureau of Foreign and Domestic Commerce. *Census of Manufactures*, 1929. Report of the United States Commissioner of Internal Revenue, 1930. U. S. Bureau of Fisheries, Document No. 1098. U. S. Department of Agriculture, Year Book of Agriculture, 1931. U. S. Census of Distribution, 1929. Social Work Year Book, 1929. Encyclopaedia of the Social Sciences, Vol. 3.

the habits of the people and created an unprecedented willingness to spend money freely for sports and amusements. There can be no doubt of the recent trend away from the more simple and less expensive leisure time pursuits to those that are more costly. Bicycles have been replaced by automobiles and canoes have given way to motor boats. Quiet vacations spent at home or in adjacent places have been supplanted by vacation motor tours covering many hundreds of miles and involving considerable financial outlay. No popular outdoor games of a generation ago required even a small fraction of the expenditures that are now made to provide facilities and equipment for the playing of golf. An important characteristic of present day recreation in comparison with that of the past is the heavy burden of expense that goes along with its enjoyment.

Any exact measurement of these mounting costs over a period of years for the entire field of recreation is impracticable because of lack of comparable data. Our estimate of the rate of increase must be limited to specific items and activities sufficiently representative perhaps to indicate general trends but by no means comprehensive. The annual production of sporting and athletic goods, not including firearms and ammunition nor sport clothes, increased nearly two and one-half times between 1919 and 1929. The production of children's toys and games during this period increased in value about one-third as rapidly as did sporting goods while the manufacture of pool and billiard tables and bowling alleys declined in value by nearly one-half.[13] Receipts from the federal tax on the dues of social and athletic clubs show an increase of about 2.4 times between 1920 and 1930 in spite of the fact that the basis of taxation was changed during this period so as to exempt many of the smaller clubs that had previously been taxed.[14] The probabilities are that certain types of clubs in this group, notably golf and tennis clubs, increased their total expenditures to a much greater extent. Applying to the golf courses

[13] *United States Census of Manufactures*, 1919, 1929.
[14] Annual Reports of the United States Commissioner of Internal Revenue.

existing in 1916 the average valuation of golf courses in 1930, the investments for golf facilities increased 8 times during this period.[15] Since this computation doubtless allows too high a value for the earlier courses, this rate of increase must be considerably underestimated. College football receipts in 1930 were more than three times the receipts in 1920. The expenditures of governmental units in the field of recreation have been increasing fairly rapidly, although no more rapidly than other government expenditures. The expenditures for the operation and maintenance of general recreation departments in 146 cities of 30,000 population or more, for which data were available, increased about seven and one-half times between 1903 and 1928. Per capita expenditures increased from $0.35 to $1.44 during this same period, but these recreational expenditures were in the same ratio to total expenditures in 1928 as in 1905.[16] The per capita expenditures of states for recreation increased from one to three cents between 1919 and 1928[17] but still remain an extremely small item in comparison with other expenditures (Table 50). The appropriations of the federal government for national parks increased 14 times between 1917 and 1930.[18] There is no satisfactory basis for measuring the increased expenditures for pleasure travel but there can be no doubt that automobile touring, which now constitutes the largest item in this field of recreation, is almost entirely a development of the past two decades and has gone forward with extraordinary rapidity since 1920. According to estimates by the United States Bureau of Foreign and Domestic Commerce the expenditures for foreign travel increased steadily from $356,000,000 in 1922 to $878,407,000 in 1929, and dropped to $829,721,000 in 1930; the increase for the entire period was 133 per cent.[19] Since the estimated attendance at moving picture theaters

---

[15] *The Golf Market* (1930 edition), published by *Golfdom*, Chicago.
[16] U. S. Bureau of the Census, *Financial Statistics of Cities*, 1928.
[17] U. S. Bureau of the Census, *Financial Statistics of States*, 1928.
[18] Annual Reports of the National Park Service.
[19] U. S. Department of Commerce, *The Balance of International Payments of the United States in 1930.*

nearly trebled between 1922 and 1930, the expenditures of the public for this form of amusement must have increased at a similar rate on the assumption that the average price of admission remained the same.[20] The fact that the total expenditures for the production of motion picture films increased two and one-third times between 1921 and 1929[21] gives further evidence of the growing costs in this field (Table 33). The expenditures for radio entertainment have gone forward even more rapidly. Between 1921 and 1929 the value of radio products increased thirty-five times (Table 35). On the basis of federal taxes paid by night clubs, cabarets, etc., the expenditures for this form of entertainment have remained fairly constant during the past decade. This conclusion, however, may not be justified in view of the difficulty in collecting taxes from all amusement places of this type, many of which may be operating illegally. The federal tax rate on admissions to theaters, concerts, etc. varied so frequently between 1920 and 1930 that this source of information is of no value in determining the changes in expenditures from year to year.[22] The budgets of the more important leisure time associations such as luncheon clubs, civic clubs, youth service associations, etc. have in general mounted upward during the past decade. One significant exception is found in the fraternal orders, whose membership since 1925 has on the whole shown a slight decline which would indicate decreased expenditures for membership dues.[23]

While the above examples cover a sufficiently wide range of leisure time activities to indicate clearly the trend toward higher expenditures, the wide variations in the changing costs of the different items make impossible any reliable estimate of the rate of increase for recreation as a whole. As a matter of fact the modern recreation movement has not gone forward in a consistent or well balanced manner.

[20] Estimates by the Motion Picture Producers and Distributors of America.
[21] *United States Census of Manufactures*, 1921, 1929.
[22] Annual Reports of the United States Commissioner of Internal Revenue.
[23] See Chapter VII for data concerning leisure time associations.

Certain forms of recreation for a time enjoy wide popularity only to be supplanted by others with a wider appeal. American recreation during the past decade has been dominated by the automobile, the moving picture, the radio, and competitive sports organized on a grand scale following patterns set by the business world. More than two-thirds of our nation's recreation bill can be charged against these forms of amusement which now occupy the center of the stage. Whether Americans will continue to give their chief allegiance to expensive types of sports and amusements it is difficult to predict. Many other forms of recreation of a simpler sort have had a less spectacular development during recent years but are apparently gaining a wider hold upon the people each year. Perhaps the necessity for retrenchment in the scale of living may give new impetus to leisure time activities that can be enjoyed at a minimum of expense.

The popularity of expensive forms of recreation must not, however, be regarded as the sole cause of the nation's expanding recreational budget. The trend toward wider participation in leisure time activities is another factor of equal if not greater importance. Vacation motor tours bulk so large in the cost of recreation because 40,000,000 people enjoy each year this form of pleasure travel. The attendance of 100,000,000 people a week is the explanation of the enormous moving picture bill of the nation. During this past decade record breaking crowds have attended baseball and football games, prize fights, horse races, and a large variety of other sports. The increasing number of participants in outdoor sports and games has made necessary an extraordinary advance in providing suitable recreational facilities easily accessible for the mass of the people. The acquirement of land suitable for modern sports has involved heavy expenditures both by municipalities and by private clubs and associations. Investments in municipal parks already total more than two billion dollars. For golf playing facilities nearly three-quarters of a billion dollars have been paid out of public and private funds. The expenditures for recreation have constantly mounted during the past decade because of the effort to keep pace with the unprecedented demand for more space and equipment for play.

It must not be forgotten also that this great advance in recreational costs occurred during a period of business prosperity when money was available for many purposes and was spent with unusual freedom. The widespread desire to enjoy sports and amusements led to rapid increases in recreational budgets that have had to be curtailed during these times of financial depression. Municipalities under the necessity of economizing have greatly reduced their expenditures for recreation. Golf and other recreational clubs have in many instances undertaken a too elaborate program and now must make drastic retrenchments. Large numbers of people have been forced by a declining income to indulge in less expensive pleasures. Apparently the curve of recreational expenditures reached its highest point in 1929 and since then has been going downward. In spite of these setbacks, however, there is no evidence of any declining interest in the field of recreation. During the coming years there may be no repetition of the spectacular growth of recreational activities that took place during the past decade but no doubt every effort will be made to provide more adequate facilities for the enjoyment of leisure. Perhaps during a period of slower development there may be greater success in building up a well balanced recreational program more carefully planned in the interests of the general welfare.

INDEX

INDEX

Industrialization, relation to recreation
  movement, 9, 10
Ingalls, W. R., 184*n*
Intercollegiate Association of Amateur
  Athletes of America, 7
Intercollegiate tennis, 68
Intercollegiate Winter Sports Union
  78

J

Jackson, L. F., 148*n*
Johnson, F. Ernest, 142*n*
Johnston, Alexander, 87*n*

K

Kirkpatrick, E. L., 150*n*
Kiwanis International, 131
Knights of Columbus, 143
Kolb, J. H., 148*n*, 158*n*
Krout, John Allen, 3*n*, 6*n*

L

Legislation, public recreation, 167
  school playground, 23
Leisure, growth of, 10
  rural, 149
Lies, E. T., 23*n*
Lindboe, Gustave E., 77*n*
Lions International, 131
Los Angeles, municipal camps, 44
Luncheon clubs, 131–134
  expenditures for, 190
  recent growth, 132
  regional distribution, 133
Lynd, R. S., and Lynd, Helen M.,
  99*n*, 123*n*

M

MacGregor, F. H., 177*n*
Masonic societies, 127–129, 160
Menke, F. G., 4*n*, 55*n*, 56*n*, 85*n*, 94*n*,
  97*n*
Middletown, sports news in, 98
Montgomery, E. W., 147*n*
Moore, Barrington, 172*n*

Motion Picture Producers and Distributors of America, 189*n*
Motion pictures, 108–112
  censorship, 176–178
  criticisms of, 111
  early beginnings, 108
  expenditures for, 109, 189
  number of theaters, 109
  in rural communities, 160, 161
  sound equipment, 110
Motor boats, number of, 54
  value, 55
Mountain climbing, 51
Municipal parks, distribution of, 28
  growth of, 25, 26
  recreation facilities, 30
  total acreage, 27
Municipal recreation, administration
  of, 168
  cost of, 185
  governmental agencies administer-
    ing, 169
  legal status of, 167

N

Nason, W. C., 162*n*, 163*n*
National Archery Association, 7
National Association of Motion Pic-
  ture Producers and Distributors,
  111
National Association of Professiona
  Baseball Leagues, 85
National Broadcasting Company, 120
National Collegiate Athletic Associa-
  tion, 87
National Conference on State Parks,
  170
National Cross Country Association, 7
National Daylight Saving Association,
  81
National Federation of Settlements,
  139
National Football League, 94
National forests, origin of, 40
  recent policies, 42
  visitors to, 41
National organizations, 137, 146
National Park Service, 38, 44, 79, 171